MATTHEW,
MARK,
LUKE
&
YOU

MATTHEW, MARK, LUKE & YOU

WILLIAM J. O'MALLEY

ave maria press AmP Notre Dame, Indiana

NIHIL OBSTAT
Rev. Msgr. Glenn D. Gardner, J.C.D.
Censor Librorum

IMPRIMATUR
† Most Rev. Charles V. Grahmann
Bishop of Dallas

June 10, 1996

www.avemariapress.com

International Standard Book Number: 1-59471-045-7

Previously published under the Thomas More ISBN: 0-88347-286-4

Printed and bound in the United States of America

To Jack Boyle, s.j.

who taught me
that you can know
and still believe.

TABLE OF CONTENTS

INTRODUCTION

Very few people claim to understand a mathematics book, especially after the first reading. All those funny symbols. Most of us just don't know the code well enough to give any opinion of the book at all. Similarly, most of us can't read through a physics text and say, "This book's stupid!" We just don't know enough about the subject and the language to have a worthwhile opinion. But I'd be rich if I had a dollar for every time students finished a play or essay or poem and said, "Garbage!"

What they mean, of course, is not that the book gives off an odor but that they found reading it puzzling, therefore unpleasant. It had nothing to say to them. But they rarely go further and ask *why* it had nothing to say to them. In fact, what they are really—and illegitimately—saying is that, because it had nothing to say to *them,* it had nothing to say at all. The cause, I think, is that those books are written in English; most of the words they've seen before, but the thing still doesn't make sense. And if the book doesn't make sense—since it's in a language they've all spoken since childhood, the fault must be with the book and not with them. The trouble is Shakespeare and the Bible are more high-powered than their readers. They use language and thought on a level the reader is not prepared for. But, like the fox in the fable, if such readers can't grab hold of them, the grapes must be sour.

According to the *Jerome Biblical Commentary:*

"Because scripture is inspired and presumably this inspiration was for the good of all, there has arisen the fallacy that everyone should be able to pick up the Bible and read it profitably. If this implies that everyone should be able to find out what the sacred author is saying without preparation or study, it really demands of God in each instance a miraculous dispensation from the limitations imposed by differences of time and circumstance."

In Shakespeare and the Bible, the author's period of time, manner of expression, and cast of thought are so far removed from our own that those books are as complicated as a math or physics book. The author's primary obligation was to be intelligible to people of his own times. And yet, in each case, he or she does have something to say to our times too, provided we are willing to give them more effort than it takes to read the sports pages or a romance novel. In order for a person to read the gospels with intelligent appreciation, one's scriptural education should be proportionate to his or her other general education. That's why this present book was written—at least to begin forming an ability to enter that treasury.

There are really two preliminary problems with approaching the gospels, the same problems one encounters when approaching Shakespeare. First, they're not straightforward prose; they are written in symbolic language; second, they are told in the form of symbolic stories. Therefore, unless gospel readers have tuned up their sensitivities to symbolism, they're going to be like people reading without their glasses. All they're going to get is a fuzzy outline of what the gospels have to say—and much of that is going to be not only out of focus but dead wrong.

Symbolic Language

Symbolic language we use all the time: "He's a bonehead; you could have knocked me over with a feather; sometimes you've got to be cruel to be kind."

We're used to most figures of speech we hear every day; we've heard them before, and if we didn't understand a particular one the first time, somebody explained it, and the next time we just do the "translation" automatically. "Bonehead" doesn't mean he's got a head made entirely of bone, and from then on it's just a synonym for "jerk." Figures of speech no longer have the power to shock—or to inform beyond the literal level.

But in Shakespeare or any other unfamiliar poetry, we come on verbally compacted sayings we've never heard before. That's why few continue to read Shakespeare or poetry after they're no longer forced to. Unraveling the confusion takes too much effort to bother with. The gospels are the same: verbally compacted poetry and stories. If someone ever explained, he or she did it too early and presumed we understood—or that we'd find it important enough to remember. And we've heard gospel passages so often we think we do understand; we confuse familiarity with comprehension.

As a result of hearing explanations of the gospels too early and too often, we never *really* hear them—not in the same way we really hear, "You've got three cavities" or "I love you, too."

The gospels don't make any *real* sense till you "decompact" them: crack them open and see what truth they carry inside.

What's more, many of the symbols the gospels use are bewildering because they're just not part of our modern culture. What's a winnowing fan? What's all this about storing new wine in old wineskins; I've never seen a wineskin in my life. "If you want the first place, take the last place"—that's impossible, unless you're the only one in the race.

Symbolic Stories

Although we're used to hearing stories, we often don't treat them as more than something to pass the time, like a sitcom or a soap opera. There's no profound meaning in them, at least not for oneself. If there is, finding it is just too much work.

But there's a difference between "entertainment" and "literature." Entertainment—most movies and TV shows, romance novels, spy stories—engage our attention awhile, hook us on a fast-moving plot or intriguing characters, and that's that: We leave them behind like empty soda cans. But although literature—the kind of "stuff" they taught in school, like *Lord of the Flies* or *Romeo and Juliet*—is trying to entertain, too, it also has a deeper purpose: to say something important about how to be a decent human being. Sometimes it compacts the principles it's trying to teach into a hero or heroine—like Jack in the Beanstalk or Cordelia ("Be like this."); sometimes it shows the truth with distorting mirrors, showing what happens to people when they defy the principles or choose a travesty of them instead—like *1984* or *The Color Purple* ("Don't be like this."). Just as symbolic language, symbolic stories have to be decompacted, or they remain mystifying and uncommunicative.

What's the author trying to say about human life *through* this story? If that's true of *Macbeth* and *To Kill a Mockingbird*, it's all the more true of the gospels—not only the stories that Jesus tells to exemplify a message but also the actual events the gospels describe. Many of them actually did historically occur, some of them did not—but nonetheless they embody a truth. That may be puzzling, or perhaps even a little intimidating, but that's the puzzle this book is trying to unravel.

Finally, people who attack the gospels as naive use the argument that they're full of contradictions. Just look at the stories about the empty tomb, for instance. One gospel writer has the women met by a young man in white, another by *two* men in white, another by an angel, another by *two* angels. Well, they certainly can't *all* be true, right? Wrong.

Method

The method this book suggests for approaching the gospels will probably be different from any other you've ever experienced. It's not going to be a homily, or a geographical tour of Palestine, or a series of precepts vacuumed out of the New Testament and handed to you on a plate.

It's meant to make *you* able to read the gospels without a teacher or homilist to do the work for you. To do that, you've got to become a word-and-story detective. You've got to come at the sayings and stories as if for the first time. Pick them up, twist them around, look behind them: decompact them. For yourself.

Detectives are very humble people. They don't jump to conclusions; they don't start with preconceptions; they don't try to dominate the evidence. They let the clues lead *them*. And they're the last ones to go by "everybody knows."

That's the only way to approach the gospels: Let the gospels say what *they* want to tell you, not the things everybody has always told you they were saying. Nor are the gospels a Rorschach test: a series of inkblots that ask, "What does this make you think of?" The authors had a definite message to communicate. You may agree with it or disagree with it, but before you can do that you have to discover just what it is the *author* wanted to say.

In order to do that, you've got to sharpen up your sleuthing skills, which is what this book is for.

Accurate vs. Meaningful

We often use words—"love," "sin," "pride," "value," "perfection," etc.—whose meanings we more-or-less understand, and yet we'd be hard-pressed to give an accurate or meaningful definition without a dictionary. Many people live long happy lives without knowing what "irony" or "symbol" really mean and how they enhance communication, but as a result, their reading of scripture is severely impoverished.

In English, most of us learned that "metaphor" means "a comparison without 'like' or 'as.'" We learned how to separate metaphors from similes on the test, then got on with the serious business of making a living. All that impractical information about figures of speech filtered down into the "Non-Current" files of our memories, along with "The area of a circle equals pi-r-squared" and "Shakespeare (1564–1616)." *Trivial Pursuit* stuff. We had an accurate, dictionary understanding of the *word,* but in many cases it had no *effect* on the depth of our reading—of anything, much less scripture. Few of us find ourselves saying, "That's a nifty little paradox! I'll have to disentangle it and see what it's trying to say."

ADAM: Not a proper name like "Sam" or Joe." Rather, it means only "the man." The root comes from the word for "earth." Therefore, it means literally "earthy one."

LIFE: The breath of the soul, a gift of the Living One.

SOUL: Life, person, self, I. To seek one's soul is to seek life.

HOLY: Fulfilling the will of God, mature moral completeness, not for fulfilling the Law but from personal and experiential knowledge of God.

SIN: *Hamartia* means literally "to miss the mark," to fail to fulfill one's purpose, to betray the love of God. It is captured by Jesus in a son wandering away from the house of his father.

ETERNAL LIFE: Not merely life in the world to come but the aliveness of the eternal God in us right now.

Why use metaphors and symbols at all? Why not just say what you mean, flat out? And what does a sensitivity to figurative language have to do with reading scripture?

The contention of this book is that you will never read scripture as the writers intended if you read the words and stories as if they were intended literally and as if the words meant the same to a first-century Jew writing in Greek as they would to someone writing English today. Take just two examples for the moment: "pride" and "perfection."

Psalm 10 says, "The wicked in their pride think God doesn't matter." Therefore, one gets the idea that to be proud is to be wicked, and thus it's wrong to feel genuine self-esteem over a job well done: "I'm grateful for the praise, but, really, I could have done far better." But the psalmist didn't mean that at all! By "pride," the psalmist means arrogance, smugness, the self-absorption which doesn't need anyone else, which says "God doesn't matter." But because of that seemingly insignificant quibbling over words—"arrogance" and not "pride"—countless good people have felt that, no matter how hard they tried, they were nothing more than unprofitable servants. What's worse, that feeling became a self-fulfilling prophecy: because they felt no honest pride in doing God's will, they did little or nothing.

Along the same line and with just as corrosive an effect, Jesus says, "Be perfect as your heavenly Father is perfect." As a result of taking "perfect" in the sense we mean now—flawless, unblemished, immaculate—countless Christians are afflicted with perfectionism. Good-enough is *not* good enough, and therefore they lead lives of wretched nit-picking or, worse, painful scrupulosity. But when a Jew like Jesus said "perfect," he didn't mean flawless, he meant *whole*. If Jesus were saying that today, he might have said, "Have your act together; know who you are and where you're going." There is only One perfect—

in the sense of "flawless": God. Trying to have God's flawlessness is not only dooming oneself to lifelong frustration—trying to achieve the unachievable—but it is also blasphemous. Perfection is precisely what Adam and Eve were after: equality with God.

Reading those two words without knowledge of what they meant to the *writer* forces the scripture to say exactly the *opposite* of what the writer intended!

Part One

THE TRUTH FROM ANOTHER ANGLE

Chapter One

LITERAL AND FIGURATIVE
LANGUAGE

For Your Consideration

Meg and Don are out for dinner. The kids are at Meg's mother's. This was supposed to have been a festive occasion, but it hasn't been a peachy day for either of them.

MEG: So, did I tell you what that cow at the check-out said?

DON: Yes, honey. About 27 times, I think.

MEG: "Right there under your nose, dearie," she said. "If it had teeth it would've bit ya. 'None so blind as those that will not see,'" she said, like she was the Queen of England. I felt two inches tall.

DON: The boss canned Dick McCurdy today. His nose has really been out of joint all month. Genghis Khan. My gut tells me I may be the next head on the chopping block.

MEG: Oh, Don, you're being a regular old woman again. Every time he looks cross-eyed, you think it's the End of the World.

DON: What a lucky boy I am: married to Ann Landers. You're all heart, babe.

MEG: I'm sorry, pal. I guess we both turned our day into "Oedipus" and "Antigone." Can we bury the hatchet?

DON: How 'bout in my boss's skull?

Now re-read the dialogue as if Meg and Don meant what they said *absolutely literally*. Pretty bizarre, right? Cows at the cash register, the boss stuffing Dick McCurdy in a can, calling your wife "Ann Landers" when you know her name is Meg? And yet you understood exactly what they meant as you read along. Why?

Here's a "translation."

MEG: Did I tell you what that irritating woman at the check-out said?

DON: Yes, dear. More than once, I think.

MEG: "You were standing right in front of it, madame," she said. "It was right there if you'd only looked down. When we don't see what's there, we might as well be unsighted," as if she were some personage. I was very embarrassed.

DON: The boss terminated Dick McCurdy's employment today. He's been unusually irritable all month. A tyrant. I have an intuition that I might be the next one let go.

MEG: You become overly upset at trivial stimuli. Every time he is irritable, you magnify it way out of proportion.

DON: (Becoming nastier) Are you some kind of know-it-all? You're not being very supportive.

MEG: I'm sorry, my friend. I guess we both exaggerated our misfortunes today until they began to look heroically tragic. Can we make peace and start over?

What's missing? Do people actually talk like this second dialogue? Not without putting one another to sleep. And why is Don's final comment about his boss's head simply untranslatable? Why is it that literal-minded people have no sense of humor?

Contrast Don's second-last speech in the first version with his last in the second version. In the second, the playwright had to insert the parenthetical note that there is a nastier *tone* than the more literal version would imply just from the words themselves. What specific different word choices did the first "Don" make that gave the reader that understanding without the clumsy parenthesis?

A

See if you remember the more common figures of speech well enough to match them up with their definitions.

A. HYPERBOLE
B. IRONY
C. PARADOX
D. METAPHOR
E. ALLUSION
F. PERSONIFICATION
G. SYMBOL

1. Comparison of two basically unlike things
2. Saying the opposite of what one means
3. Giving non-humans human qualities
4. A famous figure as a comparison
5. An apparent contradiction
6. Obvious exaggeration
7. A concrete object for an abstract idea

1.___
2.___
3.___
4.___
5.___
6.___
7.___

B

Now see if you can match up the figures with examples from the first version of the dialogue.

A. HYPERBOLE
B. IRONY
C. PARADOX
D. METAPHOR
E. ALLUSION
F. PERSONIFICATION
G. SYMBOL

1. That cow at the check-out.
2. What a lucky boy I am.
3. My gut tells me....
4. "Oedipus" and "Antigone"
5. None so blind as those that will not see.
6. About 27 times, I think.
7. Queen Elizabeth

1.___
2.___
3.___
4.___
5.___
6.___
7.___

ANSWERS: A: 1-D; 2-B; 3-F; 4-E; 5-C; 6-A; 7-G.
        B: 1-D; 2-B; 3-F; 4-E; 5-C; 6-A; 7-G.

• What does the *tone* of the first Meg-Don dialogue tell
  you that the second doesn't? About their usual relationship? What are the advantages of figurative
  language—curve-ball word-choices—over literal
  language?

Now read the following as if they were intended by the
writers to be taken literally.

• If you want the first place, take the last place.

• It is as easy for the rich to get into the Kingdom as for
  a camel to get through the eye of a needle.

• If your eye is a source of sin, pluck it out.

• The seed the sower sowed is the word of God.

• Be like the lilies of the field. They neither toil nor
  spin, but your heavenly Father takes care of them.

• John the Baptizer is the new Elijah.

How can you be first *and* last unless you're the only person
in the race?

Jesus had many well-to-do disciples: Martha, Mary, and
Lazarus, Joseph of Arimathea. If they'd given up all their wealth,
Jesus would have starved. How did they manage to squeeze
through that needle-eye?

Every Christian over twelve has looked at things that
caused lustful responses. Why are there so few blind Christians?

Seed is seed; words are words. What do the two have in
common? They're both spread around, but is that all?

All well and good for the lilies of the field, but they have their food delivered to them every day. How can I support a family standing around looking beautiful all day? Be a model?

If you don't know who the *old* Elijah was, can that statement make any sense? Can anyone read the New Testament without a basic knowledge of the figures of the Old Testament—and what they symbolized to Jewish writers and readers?

Figurative Language

Every writer knows it's better to "show" than to "tell." Writing "He was a slob" gets the basic idea across, but "His stubble looked like a mangy cat, and the rest of him smelled as bad" also does the basic job—and better.

Literal language "tells"; figurative language "shows." My dictionary takes 44 lines to define love, literally, and when I came to the end of it, I said to myself, "I wish I knew as little about love as that Noah Webster did." On the other hand, a muddy little kid at the doorway holding out a bunch of dandelions to his mother "says" love, too—and a lot better, even if a lot less clearly. The dictionary is "correct"; the boy is "meaningful."

The two versions of the dialogue between Meg and Don "said" the same things, but the first said a great deal more.

In the first place, figurative language is more interesting than literal language; the first dialogue captures the reader's attention and holds it in a way the second just doesn't. Figurative language is more fun. It gives our imaginations a workout.

In the second place, the reader "gets into" the scene, understands the emotional undercurrents. The reader sensitized to word choices and images knows something about Meg and Don that the reader of the second dialogue can only guess at: they offhandedly call one another "pal" and "babe," which the whole context of the interchange tells you is not sweetness-and-light, and yet it's not acidly sarcastic either. They're both literate people; she uses the names of two Greek tragedies and assumes he understands. They take a kind of pleasure in their own ironies and exaggerations—and in one another's. There's a lot more waiting to be discovered in the first version than in the primmer second one, but only if the reader has an ear sensitive to *tone*.

"Don't you use that tone with *me*, young lady!"

"*What* tone? I *said* I'd *do* it, *didn't* I?"

Nobody can get a court conviction based on tone of voice, only on the literal words spoken. But both the mother and the daughter know what the "tone" was, and the communication was far different from the literal words. Someone can say "Nice dress" with a sour tone that lets you know that's not what she means, but on paper one has to write, "she said, with venom dripping from her canine teeth," or "Nice *dress*. Salvation Army?"

When one reads words on a page, there's no tone of voice to judge from. Especially in something as sparely written as the gospels, we have to sense out the overtones in other ways. The gospel writers weren't writing novels in which you could judge a character's tone by his not looking in her eyes or her glaring when she italicizes: "Of *course*, I love you, *Egbert*." The gospel writers were trying to outline a message. There's no way, for instance, to know that Jesus didn't *chuckle* when he said, "It's as easy for the rich to get into the Kingdom as for a camel to get through the eye of a needle" or the look on Jesus' face when he said to Peter, "Get behind me, you Satan."

"Tone" is the literary term that sums up methods a skillful author uses to manipulate the reader's understanding. Some of those methods are word-choice (diction), figures of speech (metaphor, irony, etc.), and objects chosen. *And* each of those verbal usages has to be judged in the overall *context*. For instance, neither Meg nor Don is actually furious, which you can tell by their easygoing joking at the end. Therefore, although all alone the statement "You're becoming an old woman again" might sound harsh, in context it's far less harsh. **Word-choice** (diction) is all-important to a writer. First, every word has a *denotation*, a dictionary meaning that pretty well isolates it from designating any other object. A horse is an equine quadruped and not a bull, a bovine quadruped. "Horse" separates the two. But the dictionary definition, the denotation, is just an unsatisfying stick-figure. Language is far more nuanced than that; there are a lot of other words that focus *this* horse from *that* horse. You can sense the difference between "stallion," "drayhorse," "nag," "Bucephalus." Those overtones are the word's *connotations*—which the literal left brain can't grapple with but the imaginative right brain can "resonate" to—if it's turned on and working.

So it's important when reading the gospels to know what connotations a word had *to first-century Jews writing in Greek* in order not to be completely off-base in interpreting them. Think of the difference between our idea of "perfect" or "pride" and theirs. Furthermore, most readers will not have any facility in Greek; therefore, they can access the gospels only through the work of translators—each of whom was making his or her *own* word choices to try to get some modern English word most closely equivalent not just to the Greek word the writer chose (denotation) but, from context, what the writer *meant* (connotations).

Figures of speech (metaphor, irony, etc.) are also important for the relationship between writer and reader. "Why are you so anxious to help your brother take a splinter out of his eye when you've got a plank in your own eye?" Anyone who reads that literally comes up with nothing but gibberish: Are we talking about sinfulness here or about splinters? And how could anybody have a whole plank in his eye? "When you give alms, don't even let your left hand know what your right hand is doing." If you're insensitive to irony and paradox, you will never get a sense of Jesus' gleeful word-games.

Objects chosen set a tone, too. In John Gardner's *Grendel*, for instance, a cynical ogre hurls a "skull-sized rock" at a "stupidly triumphant" old ram and lets out a howl that makes the water at his feet turn "sudden ice." The gloom of the scene, the tone, is already set up just by the diction and objects.

Objects also reveal the speaker's sense of the audience. When people asked Jesus what in the world he meant by this "Kingdom" thing, Jesus could well have given them a literal theological treatise. (Thumb through a theological dictionary for the word "Kingdom": it'll melt your mental circuits.) No, Jesus had a fine-tuned sense of his audience; he was a genius at show-don't-tell. The Kingdom is *like* leaven in dough, a party, a treasure found in a field. But of course Jesus is powerless to communicate if the audience won't *decompact* his metaphors: discover for themselves what this Kingdom enterprise has in common with leaven, parties, and financial windfalls.

Context is also important in judging an author's choice of a word or object. Context is the background, the accumulation of all the rest of the tone and object choices in which this word's meaning is judged. Vulgar language in the context of a locker room, for instance, wouldn't raise an eyebrow. But the exact same words in the context of a cloistered convent would have quite a different effect. When Jesus bawls out the pharisees, that's one context; when he bawls out Peter, his friend, among the disciples, that's a different context entirely.

In the second half of this book, we hope to study the three synoptic (Matthew, Mark, Luke) gospel versions of the passion side by side, episode by episode, to show how the sensitive reader can see not only Jesus' choices of words, figures, and objects but how the three *differ* from one another *as authors*, making different choices of words, figures, and objects—and yet get the same idea across.

There are far more figures of speech than this book will study—perhaps 250! But separating simile from metaphor seems too picky, based merely on whether "like" or "as" is involved; they both do the same job: Explaining something less known by comparing it to something better known. We will limit our scope to three broad areas and only the six most common uses of figurative language:

DISTORTION: Hyperbole, Irony, Paradox
COMPARISON: Metaphor (Simile, Personification)
ASSOCIATION: Symbol, Allusion.

A quick overview of the figures before we study them more closely, both in ordinary usage and in the scripture:

Distortion

Hyperbole is an obvious exaggeration, saying *more* than one actually means: "About 27 times, I think; I felt two inches tall; you think it's the End of the World."

Irony says the *opposite* of what one really means; the only way to tell that is from the context: "What a lucky boy I am; you're all heart, babe."

Paradox seems at first to be a contradiction, usually depending on two different meanings to the same word: "None so blind as those that will not see."

Comparison

Metaphor compares two *un*like things, trying to explain what is less known by similarities to what is known: "that cow; canned; nose out of joint; next head on the chopping block; regular old woman."

Association

Symbol uses a concrete object to physicalize a reality that is not itself physical: "the Queen of England; Ann Landers."

Allusion is a particular use of symbols, taken from history or literature: "Genghis Khan; 'Oedipus' and 'Antigone'; bury the hatchet."

The point is *not* to read and say, "Oh my stars! That's a metaphor, isn't it!" Also many times a particular statement is a combination of several figures; "next head on the block," for instance is hyperbole, comparison, *and* allusion to history; not for fruitless academic debates over which predominates. Rather, the point is to be aware figurative language takes more work than literal language does—which is precisely its purpose: when you figure something out for yourself, you understand it.

Chapter Two

DISTORTION

For Your Consideration

The difference between hyperbole and a wild generalization is that in using hyperbole the speaker *knows* it's overblown, and a sensitive reader ought to see that. Which of the following would you say are hyperbole and which are merely wild generalization?

- It's raining cats and dogs out there.

- Never trust a guy who wears a pinkie ring.

- I am not fit to kneel and untie his sandal straps.

- People who go to church on Sunday are hypocrites.

- That face would stop a clock.

What verbal signals tell you that Washington Irving does not really mean what he says in this passage?

"Have not the Indians been kindly treated? Have not the temporal things, the vain baubles and filthy lucre of this world—which were too apt to engage their worldly and selfish thoughts—been benevolently taken from them? And have they not instead thereof been taught to set their affections on the things above?"

What do you think that each of these statements is really trying to say?

- Sometimes you have to be cruel to be kind.

- Not to decide is to decide.

- If ignorance is bliss, I've met a lot of happy people.

- Poetry is a way of saying something that can't be said.

- In marriage, two become one flesh.

Distortion

Everybody has seen a caricature—the big nose too inflated, the five o'clock shadow unnaturally heavy, the little eyes too beady. And yet the very distortion of the features gives one a new insight into the subject's character.

Everybody has seen a photographic negative—the whites where the black should be and vice versa. Yet it's the same picture from a totally different point of view, as if we are looking at this person from a world where we who seem so solid are only shadows.

If you take a familiar idea and distort it—stretch it too big, come at it from the underside, imagine its darkness and light reversed—it becomes newer, more exciting, as if you'd never really understood it fully before.

Hyperbole

Hyperbole is an *obvious* exaggeration. It says more than one really means, but like all figures of speech, it is exaggeration in service of the truth. If you say, "My head is splitting" or "I bought this dress ages ago," you don't expect to be taken literally. The enlightened listener assumes the gimmick and in a flash scales the exaggeration downward—*toward* the literal truth, but not all the way. "I worked my fingers to the bone for you" doesn't mean just "I worked hard for you"; it means "I worked *damn* hard for you (and don't you forget it!)."

The scripture uses a great deal of hyperbole, particularly in the Old Testament, and anyone who takes such statements as literally true winds up with a great many impossibilities. The bizarre apocalyptic visions of the Books of Daniel and Revelation are filled with horned monsters, wheels in the air, handwriting appearing mysteriously on a wall. The author didn't believe such things actually happened any more than

Edgar Allen Poe or Stephen King believed them. Apocalyptic scripture is in code, written by underground writers during times of persecution so that the invaders couldn't understand these prophecies of their overthrow.

When scripture speaks of the Israelites wandering forty years (a whole generation) in the desert, a literalist has to wonder why they didn't just head east. When Moses led "600,000 men, not counting women and children" out of Egypt, no one stood at the gates with a calculator, and when Jesus fed the 4,000 (or 5,000), the apostles didn't collect ticket stubs. In all those cases, the numbers are exaggerated—but *obviously* exaggerated to the particular audience for whom they were intended.

The gospel writers purposely rounded off whatever time Jesus spent in the desert (three weeks? five weeks?) to *forty* days so the knowing reader would make the comparison to Moses' forty years and see Jesus is the *new* Moses. *We* are interested in accuracy; *they* were not. It's unfair to force our preoccupations into their statements. We don't tell them what they meant.

Jesus says some heavy things about pharisees, especially in Matthew 23: "blind guides, tangled serpents, whitewashed tombs." If you take Jesus' condemnations of pharisees in the context of the whole gospel, you see pharisees who came to question Jesus are always treated with courtesy, and the pharisee Nicodemus in John 3 quite likely became a convert to Christianity.

Oversimplifiers make the same mistake with Jesus' hyperboles about riches, like the comparison of the rich man to a camel trying to get his snout through the eye of a needle. (Picture a camel trying! It was a joke!) If you isolate that statement from the context of the full gospel, you get a wrong-headed notion of what Jesus felt about moneyed people. The Lazarus family had money; if they hadn't, Jesus would have gone hungry. Joseph of Arimathea had money enough to have his own tomb; if he hadn't, Jesus would have gone unburied. The Good Samaritan had money; if he hadn't, all he could have offered the beaten man by the highway would have been kind words. Jesus was talking about rich people who can't think of anything else *but* money. To them, the gospel invitation to serve the poor is incomprehensible. "I made my own money; let them make theirs!"

Irony

When the British were troubled by the high Irish birthrate in the early eighteenth century, they feared the Irish would either overrun them or provide their masters with an unfeedable horde of wild illiterates. So the Irish-born Jonathan Swift wrote a booklet called *A Modest Proposal*. He suggested the British ought to consider the Irish a blessing! They could be bred, slaughtered, and eaten, thus solving the food problem for everybody! Swift was not advocating cannibalism; with hyperbolic irony, he was trying to show the British how inhuman they had become.

Irony is tongue-in-cheek. From the words chosen or from the absurdity of the proposal, one knows the writer or speaker means the *opposite* of what she or he says: "You're getting on my nerves; go out and play in the traffic." Irony is used to make people think—or, more often, *re*think unexamined convictions.

Inexperienced readers often haven't yet fine-tuned their ears to hear the different "tone" between ironic satire and ironic sarcasm. Sarcasm is intended to hurt: it comes from a Greek word which means "tearing the flesh." If someone sneers, "*Another* brilliant idea," you know the speaker is using irony to inflict pain. But when Don used irony in that first dialogue ("You're all heart, babe"), the context shows he wasn't trying to use it viciously. Irony is like a knife—neutral until someone uses it with an *intention*: to hurt (sarcasm) or to make people re-think (satire). Surgery is not the same as stabbing.

Not only words but situations can be ironic. For instance, King Midas in the fable is granted the wondrous wish that everything he touches will turn to gold. As so often happens, the wish turns out to be not a blessing but the opposite: a curse. He didn't foresee that when his lips touched food, it, too, would turn into inedible gold. Then his little daughter jumped into his lap, and she turned into deadly gold. Reversal.

The gospels are filled with ironies—reversals of what one might have expected. Think of how many times the disciples said to Jesus, equivalently, "You can't possibly mean that!" His whole message was ironic: "I come not to be served but to serve." When asked who was the greatest in this new Kingdom, he merely held up a child. Throughout his preaching, he kept turning the tables on his questioners, eluding their traps with a slickness any eel could envy. In the story of the good Samaritan, after a priest had passed, then a levite (part-priest, part-layman), of course the audience presumed the hero would be an ordinary Jewish layman. Nope. A Samaritan, the most detested kind of renegade from orthodox Judaism. Translated into modern terms, it would be a Nazi SS storm trooper rescuing a rabbi.

For generations the Jews had expected a warrior messiah, riding into Jerusalem at the head of a glittering army to set them free after a thousand years' enslavement. What came instead was a carpenter from the hill country, born not in a palace but in a cave, at the head of a rag-tag mob of fishermen, whores, embezzlers, and paupers. Within a week of his entry into Jerusalem to their cries of "Hosannah!" he was tried before the same mob shouting, "Crucify him!" The soldiers who scourged him mocked him, shouting, "Hail, King of the Jews!"—and yet with a double-twist, their ironic sarcasm was the ironic truth. The messiah didn't mount the throne of David but a cross, crowned not with gold but thorns, to die a death reserved for runaway slaves. He was not the messiah-priest they expected, but ironically the offering, slaughtered by the priests of his day. He was himself the embodiment of God, whom God's very priests rejected. And in the sublimest of ironies, Jesus fooled them all. He came back.

In serving Christ, we serve one who conquered by his sheer impotency. Now there is irony, indeed.

Paradox

While hyperbole distorts the truth by exaggeration, and irony distorts the truth by showing its opposite, paradox distorts the real truth by making it sound contradictory.

A contradiction is a logical impossibility: dehydrated water, for instance. Common sense says the two just can't coexist. That's what paradoxes are teasing: our common sense.

The difference between a contradiction and a paradox is that, when you manipulate the puzzle, you can find the key, often a word used in two different senses. "Sometimes you have to be cruel to be kind": What appears cruel at the moment to the "victim" is actually for his or her benefit in the long run. "Not to decide is to decide": If you don't make a choice to do something, you've automatically "chosen" to do nothing.

Jesus used paradox repeatedly. When Nicodemus, a pharisee, came honestly inquiring about Jesus' doctrine, Jesus said, "Unless you be born again, you cannot enter the Kingdom of Heaven." Nicodemus reacted in shock (we don't, because we've heard it too often): "How can a grown man be born again? Can he return again to his mother's womb?" Bit too literal a mind. But Jesus was using "birth" in two different senses: physical birth and spiritual birth. When we freely accept our own baptism, we truly enter a whole, new, infinite "world."

The problem is that, even more than with other figures of speech, people get thrown by paradoxes—probably because they take more effort to disentangle. Like complex sections in Shakespeare, we look at the paradox a few seconds and then trot off to something easier.

If you want the first place, take the last place. Nothing simpler: There are *two* races, each heading 180 degrees opposite to one another. One is the race toward what Jesus called The Kingdom, the other race is toward what St. Paul called "The World." In the World Race, Mother Teresa is pretty close to dead last, but in the Kingdom Race she's pretty close to the front. The trouble is—and here we encounter the same irony we saw before—what *we* think is important is quite often more influenced by the World than by the Kingdom. Would you rather be a genuine millionaire or a genuine saint? Nifty question.

Happy are the poor, for yours is the Kingdom of Heaven. Again, subversion of expectations. We are led to believe (by the World, again) "happy" means "feeling good." On the contrary, the Greek word for "happiness" is *eudaimonia*, which means literally "a good soul." Not "*feeling* good" but "*being* good." By that definition, those who face their poverty with dignity and honor are happy; those who exploit their own fortunes out of the misfortunes of others are not happy, just "feeling good."

If you want to be a follower of mine, you have to renounce yourself. The key is again two different meanings to the word "yourself," the World's meaning and the Kingdom's meaning. To the world, the self has become more a matter of external image than internal substance, more a matter of personality than of character. Many people think "I am what I think others think of me," rather than a self one accepts, warts and all, and gets on with the matter of serving others. Self-forgetfulness is no threat to genuine self-possession.

Unless you lose your life, you will never find it. That is surely not an invitation to suicide, literal or figurative. Still again it is nearly a perfect echo of the other paradoxical challenges to what the World says is important and to what the Kingdom says is important. Check yourself out: Does "a successful life" mean to you money, fame, sex, and power? Or does it mean making a positive difference in the lives of those around you, especially those who feel helpless? Another nifty question.

Chapter Three

COMPARISON

For Your Consideration

A metaphor (simile, personification) puts side by side two unlike things which are partially similar, e.g., a heart and a pump. Then it explains a less known object by analogy to the better known object. But it doesn't work unless the listener *decompacts* it, until he or she can say, "Oh, yes. I see now."

For instance, you've never met Alfie. Well, Alfie came to dinner last night, and he's a real pig. Just with those three letters, P-I-G, a picture immediately snapped on in your mind. Now Alfie and a pig are basically unlike; the two aren't twins; Alfie has a rational mind, and he doesn't have a curly tail. But the metaphor at least brings him into better focus.

ALFIE   :   PIG
(Less known)   (Better known)

unclean
bristly
self-absorbed
dixie-cup nose
bad table manners
unexpected snorts

You might want to try decompacting the following pairs; showing what they have in common. Use the same diagram as above if it helps.

- a crossroads and a career choice

- clichés and fine wines

- cats and curious people

- war and hell

- a young tree and an adolescent

- you as a Christian and yeast

- you as a Christian and salt

- Mass and a meal

- the Christian community and a lamp in a doorway

- the end of life and a harvest

What do you think the writers are trying to say through each of the following comparisons?

- It is with words as with sunbeams—the more they are condensed, the deeper they burn. (Southey)

- The pen is mightier than the sword. (Bulwer-Lytton)

- The green lizard and the golden snake, Like unimprisoned fires, out of their trance awake. (Shelley)

- Is this the face that launched a thousand ships? (Marlowe)

- The tawny-hided desert crouches watching her. (Thompson)

- The Kingdom of God is like a mustard seed.

- The Kingdom of God is like a net filled with 156 different fish.

- The Kingdom of God is like a field of wheat in which an enemy has sowed weeds.

- Truly understanding the Kingdom of God is like finding a pearl beyond price, a lost sheep, a lost coin.

- Jesus is both the Lamb of God and the Lion of Judah.

Reflect for a moment, think how you would explain:

- an airplane to an aborigine ("Silver bird" is too easy.)

- death to a small child

- the color green to a blind person

- self-forgetfulness to a self-absorbed friend

- human fellowship to a racist

- honesty to an angry ghetto kid

- the Eucharist to a non-believer

- the afterlife to a child

- chastity to a sexually active person

- that real love is not a feeling to a romantic.

Metaphor

Figures of speech try to explain a view of life the audience finds difficult to grasp or which they've never experienced—like describing green to a blind person as chewing mint leaves and sucking the juice. Like describing what being Christian means.

Jesus said finding the Kingdom is like finding a treasure in a field. We've heard it so often without really hearing it. The statement lost its ability to provoke an "Aha!" The metaphor is useless in focusing the Kingdom unless we decompact it.

All right, there you are bopping along in your field, and your toe hits something. Hm. So you get down and scrabble away the dirt and lo! it appears to be a big wooden chest. You grab a rock and bang off the rusty lock. Slowly you creak up the lid, and wow! The box is *filled* with diamonds and rubies and emeralds and gold! And it's all *yours!* I don't know about you, but I know the first thing out of my mouth would be "Holy (*beep*)!"

So much for the treasure half of the analogy. What does it say about being a Christian? It means (according to Jesus, who should know) if you haven't appraised your being a Christian and said, "Holy (*beep*)!", you haven't found the Kingdom of God yet. Perhaps you were baptized, but you are in the Kingdom of God as Helen Keller was among loving people, before Annie Sullivan came. There, but unaware. Unnerving? I suspect Jesus meant it to be.

Extended Metaphor

That last paragraph introduced something more complex than a one-to-one metaphor. A baptized but as yet unconverted Christian is to the Kingdom as the young Helen Keller was to loving people. Like the old SAT verbal analogies. It, too, needs decompacting.

UNCONVERTED : KINGDOM = HELEN KELLER : LOVING PEOPLE

Until Annie Sullivan came along with her irritating fiddling with Helen's hands, Helen thought she knew the limits of reality. She'd worked out a pattern throughout the house so she knew where the harmful objects were, like chairs and stairs; if anyone had rearranged the furniture, she would have been devastated. But more important, since she had gone deaf and blind as an infant, she still responded to other people as autistically as an infant. As far as she knew, *she* was the only person in a silent world. All she knew came through her senses of smell and touch.

Then Annie burst into her secure solitude, refusing to content herself with teaching this little beast table manners. She was going to crack open that safe, dark, self-centered little world and let the great world come flooding in. For months, Annie wrestled with her, forcing her hands to remember the signs she didn't comprehend. Then finally, in that moment at the pump, Helen made the miraculous connection: Things have names! I'm not alone! There's a whole *world* out there I've never dreamed of! And I can *communicate* to other people through this game in the hands! Shedding the secure darkness set her free.

That's what conversion feels like. Reread the paragraph, substituting yourself for Helen and the Christian community for Helen's family. If you haven't felt that exhilaration of your whole "universe" cracking open, you have a great thrill waiting! If you're willing to let go of the secure cocoon.

"Someone is coming, more powerful than I. . . . His winnowing fork is in his hand to clear his threshing floor and gather the wheat into his barn; but the chaff he will burn in unquenchable fire" (Luke 3:15–17). [Author's translation]

The metaphor was immediately clear to anyone in Jesus' audience. They knew that a winnowing fork was a big scoop, that threshing is separating grains from stalks, that chaff is grain husks and stalks. But for someone unacquainted with Palestinian harvesting customs it remains pretty murky. When you find such passages, just look in a good biblical commentary, like the *Jerome Biblical Commentary,* which is available in nearly any library. This is its entry on verse 17.

[17]The winnowing fork: The imagery of winnowing wheat is a frequent one in the Bible for separation (purification) and fiery judgment (Isaiah 29:5–6; 41:16; Jer 15:7). With a wooden shovel the Palestinian farmer tossed the crushed stalks of wheat into the air. The heavier grain fell quickly to the ground, while the lighter chaff was blown by the wind to the edge of the threshing area, where it was gathered and later burned.

Such commentaries are invaluable, not only to the beginner at scripture but to experts. And they have explanations of every single segment of the Old and New Testaments.

"What is the Kingdom of God like?. . . It is like a mustard seed a man took and threw into his garden; it grew and became a tree, and the birds of the air sheltered in its branches. . . . It is like the yeast a woman took and mixed with three measures of flour till it was leavened all through" (Luke 13:18–21).

If you did not know that the mustard seed is the smallest of seeds, which grows into a huge bush eight to twelve feet high, or what yeast does to dough, you would miss the point: the Kingdom begins hidden and small, but eventually it grows way out of proportion to one's expectations looking at it at first. But it shelters all kinds of birds (converts) and feeds many (you might miss the fact that the woman is using a whole *bushel* of flour!).

It's interesting to notice that Luke is the only gospel writer who says the man threw the tiny seed "into his garden." Luke got the story from his copy of Mark who says nothing of a garden. Thus Luke's editorial change betrays him as a city fellow and not a native of Palestine: Mustard bushes didn't grow in gardens but rather grew wild around the Lake of Galilee.

Parables

We will return to parables later, but it is important to make the point here that parables (and any other serious story) are *stories that act like metaphors.* They try to explain a truth about human life that is less known (or actually repellent to the audience) by comparison or analogy to something better known.

Often when I'm teaching, I run up against a topic for which I know my audience has an automatic and seemingly impregnable resistance: welfare, homosexuality, the psychological effect

of most rock lyrics, extramarital sex. The usual arsenal won't
work: logical deduction, diagrams, a broadaxe. At that point, I
invariably fall back on the sure-fire method to (1) hook their
interest, (2) end-run their resistance, and (3) let them discover
for themselves, from the inside, what I'm trying to say.

I tell a story.

For instance, almost everybody admits—at least in theory—
love is more important than sex. But when it comes to actual
practice, watch out!

> *They:* You just don't understand; we love one
> another!
>
> *I:* But do you really know what love means?
> I thought I knew what love meant when I
> was. . . .
>
> *They:* Oh, it's no use arguing with you!
>
> *I:* But you've been more vulnerable to him
> (her) than you've been even to your parents.
>
> *They:* Only somebody with no heart could bring in
> logic about a subject so personal.

—etc.

Backed into a corner, I go for my last weapon: a story that
makes them pause and reflect on what they don't want to be true.

I was a breech birth, which means I came into the world
folded in half, not headfirst but rear-end first. As a result, my
mother was so torn by the delivery she had to have a great
many stitches. The doctor told my father he should stay out of
bed with her for about three months. But my father, the kindest
man, didn't want to take the slightest risk of causing her even
the slightest pain. So he stayed out of bed with her for a year.

Now: Which way did he show more love for her—by getting into bed with her, or by staying out of bed? Is it possible there's an even greater way of showing love than sex?

It's rare the story doesn't make everyone rethink—if only till the example is over—that there might be an aspect to genuine love one hasn't thought of before. At those moments, Helen Keller is getting close to the pump.

It doesn't have to be a story that actually happened, as in the case of Helen and Annie, or my mother and father, just as long as it is true-*to-life*.

We think the difference between true stories and false stories is the same as between nonfiction and fiction. Not so. One decides whether a story is true, not by whether it actually happened or not, but by whether it tells truth or not.

The story of the prodigal son, for instance, never actually happened. It's not the story of an actual flesh-and-blood boy whom Jesus knew as well as I knew my parents. Jesus made it up *in order* to illustrate a point which his audience seemed to have trouble grasping: God takes us back, with no need to grovel and no need to make restitution—as long as we come home. In fact, God doesn't even give us a penance; God gives us a party!

Even a made-up story is true—if it tells how things really are for people trying to be human.

A fictional story is false only when it tells how things really are *not*—like most of the fictional stories on TV. Most real cops never fire their revolvers; most real lawyers don't put their entire staff on one client as Perry Mason does; most real doctors don't go chasing after patients if they leave the hospital too early; most prostitutes aren't as pretty as even the ugliest on cop shows. There is more truth in most "Star Trek" episodes than there is on any soap opera.

Although we will return to parables later, one parable brings out very clearly why Jesus the Teacher returned to parables (extended metaphors) so frequently:

"There was a lawyer who, to disconcert him, stood up and said to him, 'Master, what must I do to inherit eternal life?' He said to him, 'What is written in the Law? What do you read there?' He replied, 'You must love the Lord your God with all your heart, with all your soul, with all your strength, and with all your mind, and your neighbor as yourself.' Jesus said, 'You have answered right; do this and life is yours.' But the man was anxious to justify himself and said to Jesus, 'And who is my neighbor?'" (Luke 10:25–29).

Don't pass too quickly over this opening framework to the actual story or you will miss the whole point. Notice the questioner is a "lawyer," an expert in the Mosaic Law, a learned but often too literalist theologian who has spent many years poring over the Scriptures to find the truth about how people can best live their lives. And with a surprising ironic reversal (which you will find common in the gospels), this learned theologian is in this case addressing his question to Jesus, a wise man without doubt but in the eyes of such a scholar strictly a layman, even though he flatters him with the title "Master."

What is also clear is that he already has the answer to the question of how to fulfill himself: Love God, love neighbor. His problem, though, is that despite all his literal "book knowledge" —perhaps even because of it—he still has a dispute in his mind over application to particular cases. Now any grade school student has been told that the pharisees and lawyers of Jesus' time filled their days with what we would call nit-picking and hair-splitting about particular applications of the law. For example, "If I have to give 10 percent of all I own to the temple, must I also give 10 percent of the weeds in my yard?" Sounds silly perhaps, but they went beyond that to discuss which weeds had value enough as spices that they would have to be tithed! This caricature is not at all fair. At least one major motivation behind the pharisees' scrupulous care in interpreting the law was to be sure that the good Jew was not too severely limited by blanket prohibitions.

The question here, however, is different, and it surely was a question which the learned men found troublesome, namely: If I have to love my neighbor, how far do I have to go? At any rate, the various sects in Judaism at the time differed on who could be excluded from the divine command to love one's neighbor. Almost all agreed that the term "neighbor" was restricted to their fellow Jews, but as Joachim Jeremias says in his book on the parables, there was great disagreement about which Jews could safely be excluded from the command to love the neighbor.

> "Pharisees were inclined to exclude non-Pharisees; Essenes required that a man 'should hate all the sons of darkness'; a rabbinical saying ruled that heretics, informers, and renegades 'should be pushed into the ditch and not pulled out,' and a widespread popular saying excepted personal enemies ('You have heard that God said: You shall love your fellow-countrymen; but you need not love your enemy,' Matthew 5:43). Hence Jesus was not being asked for a definition of the term 'friend,' but for an indication as to where, within the community, the limits of the duty of loving were to be drawn. How far does my responsibility extend?"
>
> Jeremias, *The Parables of Jesus*

The lawyer's real question, then, is not who is neighbor, but rather who is *excluded* from "neighbor." Had Jesus given him the answer: "You can't exclude anybody, even the hateful," the lawyer would have walked away in disgust. So Jesus told a story to *show* his answer. Keep several questions in mind:

- Excluding the robbers and the innkeeper, there are four characters in the story. From whose point of view is the story told? That is, who is present in the story from beginning to end?

- After the priest and Levite (one designated to help in the temple, like a deacon) have passed, whom would the audience have naturally expected to be the third passerby?

- How does Jesus very subtly change the lawyer's question?

- Is this story merely a fictional diversion or is it true?

"'A man was once on his way down from Jerusalem to Jericho and fell into the hands of brigands; they took all he had, beat him, and then made off, leaving him half dead. Now a priest happened to be traveling down the same road, but when he saw the man, he passed by on the other side. In the same way a Levite who came to the place saw him, and passed by on the other side. But a Samaritan traveler who came upon him was moved with compassion when he saw him. He went up and bandaged his wounds, pouring oil and wine on them. He then lifted him onto his own mount, carried him to the inn and looked after him. Next day, he took out two denarii and handed them to the innkeeper. "Look after him," he said, "and on my way back I will make good any extra expense you have." Which of these three, do you think, proved himself a neighbor to the man who fell into the brigands' hands?' 'The one who took pity on him,' he replied. Jesus said to him, 'Go, and do the same yourself'" (Luke 10:29–37).

The only character in the story to witness all that happens is the victim. He is the one Jesus wants the audience to identify with throughout the tale. There he is, ambling along the road alone when suddenly he's set upon, stripped, beaten, and left for dead. As he lies there battered and helpless in a wilderness ditch, he is aware first of a priest of his religion and then a layman in service to the Temple staring down for a moment, then hustling along. Each time a shape appears against the sun, a flash of hope. Then despair. Then a third shadow falls on him.

Think of the reactions of Jesus' audience just at that point. (Unlike ourselves, they had never heard the story before.) Such stories always have three actors: a priest, a rabbi, and a minister; a Franciscan, a Dominican, and a Jesuit; etc. So there must be a third to give the punch line. If the listeners were laypeople, they might quietly grin, seeing the high and mighty priests taken down a peg or two; after a priest and then a "lay-priest," who else could they expect in the logical progression but ordinary laypeople like themselves? On the other hand, a priest or Levite in the audience would be boiling mad.

Reversal of expectations again. The rescuer is not not even a Jew! In fact, he is worse even than a Roman. He's a half-breed Samaritan—a "son of darkness," a "heretic, informer, and renegade" who *deserved* to be "pushed into a ditch and not pulled out!" Some of his attackers called Jesus "Samaritan" when they accused him of being empowered by Satan (John 8:48). These people were a primarily Gentile people, descendants of foreigners who were settled in Israel after the deportation of the Israelites. They were considered collaborators with the invaders, both the Persians and especially with Alexander the Great who granted them the unheard-of privilege of building their own temple on Mt. Gerazim—an affront to the one true Temple in Jerusalem. Judeans and Galileans harbored an irredeemable bitterness toward the Samaritans whose territory separated them.

The combination of "good" and "Samaritan," then, was a contradiction in terms. Jesus might as well have made the hero of his story a leper, or a prostitute, or a tax collector!

Since we all at least pretend to be without prejudice, it's hard to get a modern equivalent for this object of *universal* Jewish hatred—whom Jesus pictures as the ideal son of God. A North-Irish Protestant praised before North-Irish Catholics? Martin Luther King held up for admiration at a neo-Nazi meeting? Choose the "type" you secretly most despise and hear Jesus saying, "He's the one! He is the true Christian because he sacrifices for another, in fact for one who despises him!"

It was an answer a Jew would choke on. The possibility that this detestable outcast is a hero is so distasteful that when Jesus asks who proved himself the true neighbor, the lawyer cannot even bring himself to say "the Samaritan." He can only grumble, "The one who took pity on him."

Only those in Jesus' audience who are as much outcasts as Samaritans—the poor, blind, lepers, tax collectors, whores—are untouched. Only they can whisper, "Give it to 'em, Jesus!"

And a major point of the story is lost if the reader does not see the story from the victim's point of view. In the story, he is purposely nameless, faceless—so that we "upright Jews" can put ourselves in this victim's place. *Which is precisely what the Samaritan did!* In that ditch he saw someone as outcast as he himself! As we pass along our own roads, each of us in our own way is blinded or limping or battered, victimized by our surroundings or our own inner weakness. The true neighbors are those who can see their own need reflected in the needs of those around them and say, "Our weakness makes us brothers and sisters. How can I help?" In so doing, they begin to understand what loving one's neighbor "as thyself" means. And in proportion to the way we treat those by the side of our road, acknowledging our shared weakness, Jesus will treat us as he passes near us.

You can see how Jesus subtly changed the lawyer's question. "Who is my neighbor?" becomes "Who proved to *be* a neighbor?" "Who must be loved?" becomes, more to the point, "Who is loving?" And the answer, as even the lawyer—seduced by the story—is forced to see: those who act like the Samaritan. He does not stop to consider whether he should help his enemy (if the Jew hates the Samaritan, it's mutual), or even whether this Jewish victim deserves his help. He does not count the cost or anticipate a reward. Contrary to all norms of "sensible behavior" which all men and women of the world accept, the good man acts.

In many ways, the Samaritan is like Jesus. It was to the crippled, the blind, the sinners, the outcasts—all those who "need a physician"—that Jesus instinctively went. But Jesus was and is an alien in the worldly lives of people. He is one from whom even the bitterly lonely, the cripplingly selfish, do not expect help. In fact they do not even want his help, since it would involve an admission of weakness, a dependence on him.

Is this story merely a fictional diversion or is it true? Even if it is "made up," does it say something universal of all men and women, whether in Palestine 2,000 years ago or in our world today? Only each listener can answer that question for himself or herself. That's what parables are for.

Chapter Four

ASSOCIATION

There are a lot of realities very important in our lives which are real but not visible: hope, being Irish, love, achievement, faith. But we are very physical beings; we have to *concretize* these real-but-abstract realities into physical symbols: an anchor, green, a valentine or a diamond ring, a diploma or a trophy, attendance at Mass.

For Your Consideration

There is a natural symbolism (because of the connotations) in objects which make them able to embody a truth that is real, but not physical. What are the associations we have with each of the following pairs of physical objects which make them more fitting to say one thing rather than another?

rose vs. lily

lion vs. panther

candle vs. lightbulb

sun vs. moon

oak vs. willow

engagement ring vs. wedding band

gold vs. lead

photograph vs. portrait

athletic letter sweater vs. senior ring

In each of the following groupings, which one would you think NOT to be a good unifying symbol? More importantly, why?

- Car: (A) Triumph; (B) Bullet; (C) Valiant; (D) Snail.

- Basketball: (A) Blazers; (B) Bullets; (C) Dribblers; (D) Howitzers.

- Baseball: (A) Hornets; (B) Wasps; (C) Fruit Flies; (D) Stingers.

- Men's Deodorant: (A) Brut; (B) Polecat; (C) Hunk; (D) Musque.

- Athletic shoes: (A) Cheetahs; (B) Gazelles; (C) Zephyrs; (D) Tortoises.

These two poems are about roses—and more than roses. What are the associations we have about roses (no matter our culture)? Which of the poems leaves the interpretation of the meaning of the symbols more "open" to the reader, more intriguing? How?

THE WHITE ROSE

The red rose whispers of passion
And the white rose breathes of love;
Oh, the red rose is a falcon,
And the white rose is a dove.
But I send you a cream-white
    rosebud,
With a flush on its petal tips;
For the love that is purest and
    sweetest
Has a kiss of desire on its lips.

—John Boyle O'Reilly

THE SICK ROSE

O Rose, thou art sick!
The invisible worm
That flies in the night,
In the howling storm,
Has found out thy bed
Of crimson joy,
And his dark secret
    love
Does thy life destroy.

—William Blake

Anyone who not only can identify each of the following literary and historical personages but also tell what symbolic associations they call up in the well-read mind will receive either the full Great Books Collection or a flame-colored Camaro.

Helen	Barnum	Narcissus
Boanerges	Adonis	Jezebel
Caligula	Elijah	Ruth
	Prometheus	

Symbols

- Natural symbols have cross-cultural associations.

- Their meaning is limited by their use in context.

- They physicalize real but invisible entities.

Every object has qualities and connotations of its own which give it a particular meaning. But some objects, persons, and events have such an *intensity* of consistent associations in our minds that they also stand for something else, something important that recurs in human life. These are *natural symbols*. For instance, roses are beautiful, fragile, and alive; so is love. So we give roses as a symbol of the love. The roses are not the *same* as the love, so that—when the roses die, my love has died; for the moment they serve as a physical embodiment of my real but invisible love. Lilies call up connotations different from roses. They are white, shaped like trumpets, and bloom in the spring near Easter. So they are associated with the resurrection and so are used as symbols of hope at wakes and funerals.

Image/Metaphor/Symbol

Red somehow resonates with love and passion, but also danger, heat, shame, anger, etc., which are all "hot." Its meaning in any particular situation depends on the context. For instance, when I say, "The red roses are blooming in the garden," there is no hint that I mean any more than just the plain, literal statement: an *image*. But if I say, "The red roses are blooming in your cheeks," I'm obviously not saying there are two thorny flowers literally emerging from under your eyes. Nor am I saying, "Good grief, is your face red!"; the "rose" part softens that, makes a more delicate statement. It's a figurative association between fragile, beautiful red roses and your fragile, beautiful rose cheeks: a *metaphor*. But if I say, "Every red rose blooms awhile, then fades and falls and is no more," the ponderous way I describe the life of a relatively unimportant flower gives a hint that I'm talking about something far bigger: Every living thing—including ourselves—blooms, ages, then dies. I've made the red rose a *symbol*.

Look again at the previous two poems. It is easy to see what each of the three roses means in the first poem (O'Reilly): sexual passion, pure and non-possessive love, and the pure love which nonetheless cannot deny its desire. The poem is clear and in that sense "closed"; one cannot legitimately say that the red rose in the poem means the House of Lancaster and the white rose means the House of York, or that the red rose means communism and the white rose means democracy. The poet hasn't left you that option; he's told you the limits of the symbol. If you want the roses to mean something else, you'll have to write your own poem.

But the rose in the second poem (Blake) is not so clear. It has all the associations we naturally apply to roses: fresh, fragile, rich-colored, and the added associations given it by "thy bed of crimson joy" and "dark secret love." But the poet has not limited the legitimate interpretations of the rose symbol. And the mystery is increased by the fact that the fresh and fragile rose is sick, and the cause of its sickness is the puzzling "invisible worm" whose home is "in the night, in the howling storm" and whose love is a love which destroys. Context.

Is the rose love and the invisible worm jealousy? Possibly. Is the rose innocence and the invisible worm the corrupting influence of experience, which we know was a favorite theme of Blake's? Is it humanity corrupted by Satan, or youth corrupted by time? All of them are possible, and since the poet has not given any hints at what specific corruption he was speaking of, the reader can apply it to any corruption. The only limit the poet puts on it is that this is a corruption and not some kind of happy rebirth. The poem itself won't allow such interpretation.

This point is worth making since, in teaching Robert Frost's well-known poem "The Road Not Taken," I have heard angry howls when I would admit that, yes, the choice he symbolizes by a fork in a road could mean his choice of being a poet, but it can't be restricted to that. It could be the choice of a spouse or a religious vocation or whether or not to go to war. The poem is not about *a* choice; it is about *any* choice.

Similarly, in the parable of the Good Samaritan, the victim by the side of the road does not restrict the Christian to helping only people who have been beaten and robbed, but calls on the Christian to help any one in any need. It is not the literal details which are the truth; it is the story which is the truth.

Therefore, the second assertion we can make about symbols is that their meaning is limited by their use in the context of this particular story or poem or speech.

Third, a symbol is the visible sign of something invisible. Love, for instance, is invisible. You can't give someone a basket of it or weigh a pound of it; you can't heft it, touch it or sniff it. And yet we all know that love does exist. But how can we, who are used to dealing in tangible, visible, quantifiable things, speak of something important but intangible? Well, we simply talk of love *as if* it were something measurable, even though we know it's not, as in "I love you, a bushel and a peck." Or we send a tangible box of candy or a dozen roses or a partridge in a pear tree to stand for (to symbolize) our love. It is a visible sign of something invisible-but-real. Or, as we saw above, we speak of physical things associated with our love, like our quickened heartbeats—and thus the valentine is born!

In the Bible, symbols are often used to describe experiences not only invisible like love, honor, the meaning of life, but which practically defy any capsulization in literal human speech.

They describe communications from God, for instance. God is not merely beyond time and space; God is unlimited by time and space. God doesn't wear a watch. In God's way of existing, there is no difference whatsoever between now and then or between here and there. God is timeless, everywhere. If God wants to "send a message" to someone on earth, God doesn't have to suit up and hop a spaceship from beyond the boundaries of the universe and zoom down (or up) to earth. God's here already.

Nor need God send an angel on the excuse that the Almighty is too busy or far away. And even if God did, the angel would hardly "look" like the angels we're used to seeing in pictures— a kind of sexless man/woman draped in brocade with huge feathered wings growing out of his/her shoulders. When Luke's gospel says Gabriel announced a message to Mary, even Luke didn't picture some winged creature flapping across the endless depths of space from heaven to Nazareth. One can just see him/her panting into Mary's kitchen and saying, "Look, lady, I've got a message for you, but just let me catch my breath! Whoo! That was a trip!"

Now I'm not saying there are no angels. I'm merely saying that if there are angels, they don't look anything at all like the winged creatures we picture in paintings and Christmas cards. They didn't need wings to get to Bethlehem on Christmas any more than the Son of God needed wings for the same "journey." Nor am I saying that we should necessarily drop such pictures from our Christmas cards—any more than I'd say drop the hearts from valentines. Pictures of angels with haloes and wings "say" messenger of God just as adequately/inadequately as pictures of hearts "say" love. Symbols are bound by their very nature to be only an attempt at physically approximating a reality which is far too big for any words or any picture. Angels and hearts have stood for very important realities for endless years, and until someone comes up with better symbols, there is no harm in them. In fact there is a great help in them when we try to visualize what is unseeable-but-real.

The problem is that many lock onto the symbol as if it *were* the reality—seeing, for instance, the bright-winged angel without dealing with the shattering reality of God's message breaking through into time and space. Others with similar minds argue that—if they can prove (which they can) that feathery creatures from across the gulf of space are non-existent fabrications of the imagination (which they are)—they can automatically prove (which they cannot) that messages from God don't exist.

Both fundamentalism—which is very, very religious—and scient*ism* (not science)—which is very, very anti-religion—ironically both read scripture with the same literalist eyes. Both claim that the scripture writers meant exactly, unequivocally what the words literally mean. Therefore, on the one hand, fundamentalism is stuck with believing a truckload of impossibilities which fly in the face of everything we know about science. On the other hand, scientism wipes out everything in the scriptures as total nonsense. Neither is right, because both blind themselves to the fact that metaphors, symbols, and symbolic stories tell the *truth*—provided one is willing to consider them not merely with the factual, analytical left brain but also with the intuitive, imaginative right brain. To read scripture only with the left brain is to read it half-wittedly.

The real question is not whether the symbol exists literally as we picture it, but whether the reality the symbol is trying to convey exists—in this case, whether messages from God exist. Again, since time began, men and women have had the unshakable conviction that God has communicated to them. I myself have had that experience, more often than I deserved. But how to describe it? It was like . . . like being taken outside myself. And yet that's not right; I wasn't even aware of myself. And yet I was. I mean, it was God and me, but I wasn't important. And yet I've never felt more important in my whole life. Well, maybe it was sort of like everything was filled with light. I don't mean I saw light, but it was the way I would feel if . . . .

You see how confusing it can get!

And yet it happened, and it's happened to uncountable thousands of men and women. To maintain as a foregone conclusion that it can't happen is rather like Helen Keller saying there can be no color. It is true that many people never have had this experience of God, but their lack of experience does not negate the fact that many of us actually did experience it.

But how to describe something so indescribably intense? "It was like being enfolded in wings made of light." That's not how it was, but it's somehow in the direction of what it was like. As we've already seen throughout these pages, that's what figurative language is for: to say something that literal language just can't grasp. Meg said she felt "two inches tall"; she wasn't, but she surely felt more than just insignificant. Alfie isn't a pig, but he makes me feel the way I would feel in the presence of a pig with a collar and tie on.

Think of the exercises in which you tried to explain green to a blind person or death to a young child. The same problem arises when someone who has experienced God tries to explain that moment to someone who has not experienced God.

In the same way, if you take many of the symbols of the Bible literally, you miss the whole point! They were not saying a winged creature entered Mary's kitchen; she would probably have had a heart attack on the spot! After all, seeing an angel coming down the street wasn't any more common in Nazareth than it is in Sioux Falls. And yet throwing out the reality along with the admittedly inadequate symbol is the same as (to coin a phrase) throwing the baby out with the bathwater.

If you were Moses in the desert, suddenly flooded with the presence of the uncontainable God, filling you, swirling through you, nearly drowning you, how would you describe it? I just described it with an extended metaphor trying inadequately to compare it with being drowned. The author of Exodus used precisely the opposite metaphor: fire. It was as if he were in the presence of a great fiery bush which flamed and flashed but was not consumed. You can argue that Moses did not see a burning bush, but that gives you no right to say Moses did not meet God.

If you have not had the experience of meeting God so intensely and tried to put it into words, it is difficult to describe the difficulty in describing it. It is like (and see how I have to resort to comparison even here) trying to describe the exhilaration of being in love to someone who has never fallen in love. You have to resort to anything at hand—exaggeration, comparison, association: sky-rockets, peaceful meadows, Christmas—trying to explain what someone else hasn't experienced in terms of what he or she has experienced.

St. Paul describes one of these intense moments of being with God, of breaking through from time into the timeless, as being "lifted up to the seventh heaven." The Acts of the Apostles describes Paul's first cataclysmic reaction of the truth about Jesus as being dashed to the ground by a blinding light which left him sightless for three days. The disciples described the departure of the risen Jesus, leaving them and yet somehow still with them, as his rising from the earth and moving up into the heavens. And Acts describes the return of the Spirit of Jesus as a terrifying great wind which shook the house, and as the descent of tongues of fire onto each of the disciples.

If you picture these events concretely in a painting, a one-frame freeze of the physical action (as the Scriptures do), it is not so difficult to accept; no more than the one-frame picture of a stylized and disembodied human heart on a valentine. But if you see it in motion, from the start of the event to the end, it becomes cheapened, Hollywoodized, overliteral, almost ridiculous. Certainly one can't accept it as what literally happened. Are we to see Paul at prayer or Jesus at the Ascension literally and physically lifted by some invisible force and carried through the endless miles of cold space, like spaceships in slow gear? No, but it felt like that, as one would feel *if* it had been physical rather than nonphysical, beyond words.

Was Paul physically blinded? Perhaps. It's certainly well within the realm of possibility. But the physical details are not important. They could be literal or they could be merely a symbolic attempt to put the real inner experience into words. The inner experience did happen. We have proof of that, since Saul the Persecutor did become Paul the Apostle.

Was there a wind and tongues of fire on Pentecost? Perhaps there was; perhaps there wasn't. But anyone who goes to the Jewish meteorological records of 33 A.D. and checks the storm listings or begins to analyze St. Elmo's fire or static electricity is missing the whole point! Whether the wind and fire were literal or symbolic, the disciples were—as a group and as individuals—

inspired and inflamed by an inner experience of the Spirit of Jesus. We have proof of that, since these men and women who had deserted Jesus on Good Friday and cowered in fear behind the locked doors of that Upper Room came marching fearlessly out of their security and went to their deaths unflinchingly proclaiming the reality of that experience. Perhaps they would not have died for the details of the wind and the fiery tongues, but they did die for the experience they tried to convey with those symbols. And on that experience they founded a church which—despite all the attacks from without and all the corruption from within—has endured for 2,000 years.

Perhaps it was only like a flaming bush. Perhaps it was only like a blinding light. Perhaps it was only like a great wind. But there was no doubt in their minds that it *was* God.

Allusion

An allusion is a special kind of symbol—a person, object, or event—taken from history or literature. For the most part, it works like any other symbol, but with one hitch. Natural symbols, like a rose or a wind or a fork in the road, mean about the same to any listener, no matter at what time or in what culture. But allusion depends on acquired knowledge. The figurative term—the historical, symbolic half of the comparison—is not always known to the listener. If so, not only does the allusion not clarify, it actually confuses. That's what makes reading Shakespeare and the New Testament difficult; if you know little or nothing about Greek mythology or the Old Testament, a lot of what you read is befuddling.

For instance, "Such a mind! Next thing you'll be splitting babies in half." If the listener didn't remember that Solomon, in his wise phase, solved a dispute between two women who claimed the same infant by offering to cut the baby in half, the whole point of the allusion is lost. "Solomon? Who's he play for?"

Allusions are one of the main reasons footnotes were invented. One look into a critical edition of T. S. Eliot's poems or Shakespeare's plays is proof enough of that. Most modern readers find them a pain in the neck. In the first place, it interrupts the flow of the poem or story, and in the second place it's an irritating reminder of how little one knows, like playing "Trivial Pursuit" with an expert. "Who cares what those old jerks did anyway?" Well, apparently the writers did, because to a well-educated audience, one word like "Agrippina" or "Ahab" or "Krupp" packs in whole paragraphs of associations, surrounding the here-and-now literal object or person with a whole aura of rich figurative significances. This is rather easily seen by looking at a footnote, which is usually at least three or four sentences long, and then at the allusion itself in the text, which is usually only one or two words. Like all figures of speech, allusion compacts several sentences into one or two words.

In one very important sense, the writers and readers of the New Testament were far better educated than we—for all our diversity and all our audiovisual aids. They may not have known "a little bit about a lot of things," as we do, but all of them—street sweepers, shepherds, tax collectors—knew a great deal about the events and people and symbols of the Old Testament. From their earliest years, the stories had been recited to them; when they were old enough, they sat at the feet of the village rabbi and committed hundreds and hundreds of lines of the Old Testament to memory; every sabbath they listened to a passage from the scrolls of the Torah or the prophets and heard an interpretation of the text, like a homily but longer, more detailed and more technical; old men sat on the street corners debating the meanings of verses and the requirements of the Law.

The Old Testament was their *only* library—stories and debates and songs and law and history. It was their national literature, and they all knew it well. Therefore, almost the only source of allusions in common speech and in writings for unsophisticated Jews was the Old Testament.

At the Transfiguration, for instance, the two figures who appeared with Jesus were Moses (the Lawgiver) and Elijah (the Prophet). Thus, their physical presence is exactly the same as saying "all the law and the prophets" are with Jesus—"at his side, standing by all Jesus says."

"The disciples put this question, 'Why do the scribes say then that Elijah has to come first?' He replied, 'True, Elijah is to come to see that everything is once more as it should be; however, I tell you that Elijah has come already and they did not recognize him but treated him as they pleased, and the Son of Man will suffer similarly at their hands.' The disciples understood then that he had been speaking of John the Baptist" (Matthew 17:10–13).

Therefore, the writers of the early church saw that Elijah and John were not only "sort of similar" in their ways of acting, but fulfilled exactly the same function in the plan of God: to close the Old Covenant and open the new age.

One of the most obvious types of Jesus in the Old Testament is in the Suffering Servant sections of the prophet Isaiah. As we have seen, the Jews of Jesus' time, even his own disciples, expected the messiah to be a worldly king and warrior who would drive the invaders out and reign richly in Jerusalem, as David and Solomon had. Despite all Jesus said about his inevitable suffering and the unworldliness of his Kingdom, we find him even after the resurrection still trying to get it through their heads that, if previous messiahs had been tormented by the very people they had been sent to help, all the more must The Messiah suffer, too. It had been there in the

Hebrew Scriptures all the time, but they'd refused to see it. The Scriptures showed the repeated pattern of God's dealings with God's people through messiahs, but these Jews could not divorce themselves from their hopes. Never was this pattern of ill-treatment for the messiah more clearly stated than in the prophecies of Isaiah. They are too lengthy to quote in full here (Isaiah 42:1–4; 49:1–6; 50:4–11; 52:13–53:12), but let one selection suffice.

> "As the crowds were appalled on seeing him
> —so disfigured did he look
> that he seemed no longer human—
> so will the crowds be astonished at him. . . .
> A thing despised and rejected by men,
> a man of sorrows and familiar with suffering
> a man to make people screen their faces;
> he was despised and we took no account of him.
> And yet ours were the sufferings he bore,
> ours the sorrows he carried.
> But we, we thought of him as someone punished,
> struck by God and brought low.
> Yet he was pierced through for our faults,
> crushed for our sins.
> On him lies a punishment that brings us peace,
> and through his wounds we are healed. . . .
> By force and by law he was taken;
> would anyone plead his cause?
> They gave him a grave with the wicked,
> a tomb with the rich. . . .
> By his sufferings shall my servant justify many,
> taking their faults on himself."
>
> (Isaiah 52:14–53:11)

This servant is a type of Israel itself as the ideal follower of Yahweh and particularly is he a type of the messiah-heroes who were the contact points between Yahweh and Israel: Abraham, Moses, Jeremiah, David, and especially the exiles who suffered in Babylon. But Jesus himself claimed that he, in a definitive way, fulfilled this function. He was *the* contact point between Yahweh and his people. As the other messiahs' sufferings had saved Israel from evil influences, The Messiah's sufferings would save all humankind from evil itself.

Therefore, when the gospels connect Jesus by allusion to figures from the Old Testament—Adam, Moses, David—the writers are not saying Jesus is just "another" Moses in a cycle, but that he is *the* Moses and the new Christian community is *the* Israel for which their Old Testament counterparts were preliminary stages.

Part Two

SYMBOLIC STORIES

Introduction

As kids, we really believed in Santa Claus. And in "we three kings of Orient are." We put plates of cookies out on Christmas Eve and looked on January 6 for the appearance of wise men at the crib. But then someone unmasked jolly old St. Nick and told us the wise men story was nothing but a "myth."

As we grow up, it's almost inevitable we lose our sense of awe and wonder over the simple joys of childhood. At the same time, we have not yet gotten a sense of history, the awesome realization we are a part of the great march of time which includes Alexander and Pizarro and Churchill. What we have gotten, though, is an uncritical awe at what we think is science: rock-hard proof. At least partly because of our fear of being taken in, we refuse to accept anything as true without evidence so clear and distinct there is no possibility of doubting it. It is not unlike demanding to put our fingers in the nail holes.

When we find out Santa Claus and the Magi are "myths," we feel tricked. People we trusted, like our parents, like the media, like the merchants who engulf their windows with jolly red men and elegant kings, deceived us. Everybody conspired to make us believe in a hoax. Maybe they did it to increase the fun that wonder gives to children, but they were telling a lie, right?

Not really.

Somebody did put real, tangible packages under that tree; we actually touched and tore at and eventually forgot them. Parents worked to buy the hidden presents, decorated the tree late at night, filled the stockings, ate the cookies. The jolly old man was a figure of speech for generosity: for our parents.

Similarly there was a reason why the (perhaps mythical) kings—who are nameless in the gospel, never called kings, and never restricted to three—became Caspar, Melchior, and Balthasar, one white, one black, one Oriental. Whether the event actually happened or not, the story had a very true point to make: just as Jesus came to bring his liberating message to the poor, uneducated Jewish sheepherders, he also came to share his sonship with the rich and learned Gentiles—no matter where in the world they lived and no matter of what color.

Even such sophisticated folk as prime-time news readers and *TIME* use the word "myth" only in one sense: a naive belief easily proven false, like "the myth that America could never lose a war" or "the myth that touching a toad gives you warts." But there is another legitimate use of the word "myth": a story (or a whole network of stories) which acts like a symbol. A myth tries to capture, concretely, ideas and beliefs that make the world and being human make sense—just as metaphors and symbols do.

Myth is not to be rejected because it is not historical. In fact, myth is at times truer than "the facts." Everything we saw to be true about natural symbols can also be said about myths: They are attempts to make visible a truth which is, for one reason or other, invisible. They are admittedly inadequate attempts to show what these invisible realities are *like*. They are attempts to explain what someone may not have experienced in terms of things he or she has experienced. A myth is a made-up story that is true if it tells how things really are.

The first chapters in this book had a single purpose: to show that literal language is not the only vehicle to get the truth across. It is often not even the best vehicle. In many varied ways, figurative language can communicate both the literal truth and the inner feelings the speaker has about that truth.

A myth is no more than a narrative way of trying to communicate a truth that can't be grappled with in any photo-graphic, literal way—either because the events took place at a time when no human existed capable of recording it (myths dealing with pre-history), or because the truth is too big for literal categories, not tangible (myths dealing with human meaning), or because the truth has not yet occurred (myths dealing with the future).

Myth is always trying to find ways in which to concretize truths about which we can make only *educated* guesses.

When we try to deal with pre-history—whether in Genesis, or any of the other primitive creation myths, or even in the theory of evolution—we are trying to understand events that took place before there even were human eyewitnesses. No human ever saw a live dinosaur. But they were definitely here for a long, long time; we have the bones to prove it. But no skin. We don't know what color they were. Then humans came along; again, we have the bones (far fewer than you'd guess) to prove it. But we can only make educated guesses about what they looked like, how they behaved, what they thought. A myth is story (always flawed) that tries to help us piece what little we have together into some kind of coherent whole so we can understand better.

Similarly, every philosophy and theology is a myth: a story to help us get an idea of "what it's all about." Just as we fabricate theories of pre-history from educated guesses about bones and tools, so we fabricate theories of human purpose and God's personality from looking at the way human beings and the universe are made. Although they're less academic (and therefore more accessible), folktales and fables embodying those philosophies and theologies were spun out and retold for centuries to explain life to children, especially the difficult lessons of adolescence, both the physical changes and also the new relationship with the tribe which those physical changes imposed.

Myth also helps us get at least a tenuous handle on the future. Wise folk, from Old Testament prophets to the writers of "Star Trek" to futurists like the authors of *Megatrends*, take a look at the way things are going now and—knowing how such trends ended up in the past—can make pretty educated guesses about where our choices will lead us. When a mother says, "You're heading for trouble, young man," she doesn't have a crystal ball. She's just read the story a lot more times than her son has, and she can make a better educated guess how this story will end up.

Chapter Five

MYTH AND TRUTH

For Your Consideration

In his televised discussions with Joseph Campbell, later published as *The Power of Myth,* Bill Moyers said that he was puzzled by how many times his sons had seen the *Star Wars* films. He asked them why, and one said, "The same reason you read the Bible so much."

Wisdom comes from the mouths of babes. That young man had intuited (not reasoned to) not only the motives behind his father's pondering the Bible, but the very real parallel to the effect on his own inner self of vicariously sharing the struggle between young Luke Skywalker and the Empire, focused in Darth Vader. The boy's soul resonated to that struggle, because even though his was far less dramatic (and surely less hectic!), he too faced that same struggle between good and evil within himself. In watching the films, he saw his own unrest, bewilderment, and fear *objectified,* with the sides clearly delineated. Something very good within himself understood-without-logic that Luke's story—no matter how fantastically fictional— "tells it like it is." The boy senses there is a very real but invisible "menace out there" in the faceless, anti-human world of bureaucracy, hostile takeovers, cynical and self-serving politics, athletes and entertainers whose clay feet go all the way to their heads. But he also sensed the appeal of Luke's commitment, his dignity even in defeat, his humanity..

The Evil Empire doesn't exist. But it does. It always has.

Read the following story and see what you think the story is trying to say about adolescence. What is the core metaphor, i.e., to what is the story comparing growing up? Then, what is the basic literal statement underneath that metaphor?

Once upon a time, a young man named Youth wanted to be a knight—manly, mature, sure of himself and his place in the world. His tutor, a wise but dithery old chap named Merlin, described all the adventures he'd have to endure—the Forests of Despair, the Mountains of False Delight, the Swamp of Puberty where beautiful lilies and poisonous snakes abound. On and on. But Youth was restless with dry old lectures. He wanted experience, not dusty books about people long dead.

So one day, he set out with his squire, Hope, to rescue a beautiful damsel named Perfecta, who had been locked away by the jealous witch, Time, within the dank dungeons of Castle Perilous. And the defender of the Castle was the giant, Fear, who made up for an undeniable stupidity with a strength that could pop the heads off bulls like beer caps.

Along the way, Youth and Hope had many adventures, like frequent skirmishes with Packs of wolves from the Land of Doubt. But finally they arrived at Castle Perilous, called forth the giant, Fear, and Youth engaged in hand-to-hand combat with him. Fall after fall, Youth was defeated and disgraced and retired from the fray, battered and ashamed.

But his squire, Hope, bound up his wounds, and in the company of a young man named Friend, he assaulted the giant again, and with the help of Friend and Hope, he defeated his enemy, Fear, won the heart of the damsel Perfecta, and they lived happily ever after.

Well, almost.

Try your own hand at it. (1.) Pick a literal statement about a subject you feel strongly about—and which others seem

unconcerned about. (2.) Re-state it as a metaphor. (3.) Then
spin out a story that "decompacts" that metaphor. Examples:

Lit.—A person is more important than looks.
Fig.—Beauty is only skin deep.
Story—Beauty and the Beast

Lit.—Books are a way we relive other people's lives.
Fig.—Books are doorways into fantastic new worlds.
Story—Alice in Wonderland

Lit.—"Whatever you do to the least of my brothers and
         sisters, that you do unto Me."
Fig.—All the bodies at the side of your road are your
         relatives.
Story—The Good Samaritan

What do you think Aesop is trying to say through this story?

"One day a wild boar was carefully honing his tusks on
a flinty rock when a fox ambled by.

"'Why waste your time doing that, Tusker,' the fox said.
'There's not a hunter or hound in sight.'

"'True enough,' Tusker answered, 'but when the danger
does show up, I'll have better things to do than sharpen
my weapons.'"

What truths about human life and growing up would you
say that the authors were trying teach children with each of the
following stories?

—Cinderella

—Hansel and Gretel

—Little Red Riding Hood

—Snow White

—Jack and the Beanstalk

Stories That Tell Truth

The story of Youth which opened the chapter is a made-up story, but is it true? Does it give a true picture of things as they really are? If you added more adventures that symbolically parallel the other problems of growing up, you could end up with a work like the play *Everyman* or the novel *Pilgrim's Progress*.

If you went even further and made the names less obvious and added a lot more individualizing details like the teacher's being dithery and the giant popping off bulls' heads, you'd have a novel like *The Once and Future King*. If you were even more sophisticated and less obvious, you could have a novel like *Lord of the Flies* or *Catcher in the Rye*.

All of those stories are wrapped around the same kernel of truth: adolescence is a war, and you just hope you win more battles than you lose.

Myth, then, is merely a narrative way of concretizing an abstract truth—drawing it out, unearthing as many aspects of that truth as possible. A myth is an *extended metaphor*. Along the way, there are certain positive natural symbols—damsels, squires, fellow knights, wise hermits, etc.—and many negative natural symbols—witches, giants, wolves, trolls, etc. And the struggles between them add a whole element of *entertainment* to the tale. You lure the listener to let your truth slowly seep into him or her. It sugarcoats the pill. As in the gospels, you can make the *same* point with many different stories simply by changing the governing metaphor—without boring your audience.

Fables

In a fable, the metaphor which embodies the literal truth is usually a personification of an animal. Each animal character is the type of a person—wily foxes, plodding tortoises, dumb sheep, noble horses, etc. And the literal statement—the "message"—is usually explicitly stated at the end. Here is another example from Aesop, and the fact it was written twenty-five hundred years ago shows human beings have not really changed that much.

"For years the mice had been living in constant dread of the cat. So they called a meeting to face this community problem once for all. They went round and round; nobody seemed able to come up with a plan.

"Finally, a very young mouse got up, cleared his throat. "I propose," said he, looking very important, "that a bell be hung around the cat's neck. Then whenever she's near, we'll have warning and escape."

"The young mouse sat down amidst tumultuous applause. The motion was passed almost unanimously.

"Then an old mouse with white whiskers, who had sat silent, rose and said, "Friends, it takes a young mouse to find a plan so ingenious yet so simple. I have but one question: Which one of you is going to do it?"

Application: One thing to propose; another to execute.

Such stories about animals who are like people—only simplified—have always been ways of telling children about the struggles of adult life in terms that are not realistic (since that would frighten them) but which nonetheless draw the rough outlines of what good and evil mean, how courage and cowardice fare in life, honesty and dishonesty, and on and on.

While being entertaining, such stories as Kenneth Grahame's *The Wind in the Willows* and Tolkien's *Lord of the Rings* also teach. The farm animals of Orwell's *Animal Farm* show how most revolutions end.

Folktales

Folktales are different from fables in several ways. First, they're explicitly about people, but people in situations far different from ordinary life. They inhabit an imaginary world where princes become frogs (and vice versa), a witch's apple can put the princess into a long sleep, pumpkins turn into coaches.

Folktales seem mere entertainments to put kids to sleep, or give them a sense of wonder—the joy of which we, scrabbling for sophistication, lose far too soon. But don't be fooled by their simplicity or their "unrealistic" elements. Beneath the surface, folktales are very serious indeed. They were written thousands of years ago, retold again and again, until the specifics that restricted them to one culture wore away. (*Cinderella*, for instance, began in China and thus pivots on the girl who has the tiniest feet.) Thus, the story left is universal. As much about growing up today as it was a thousand years ago.

- Folktales are trying to tell a truth.

- They are rooted in the real.

- Every one of them hinges on "The Big IF."

Truth. Folktales are very much trying to tell about the unending battle in human life between evil, which often comes from the most unexpected quarters, and good, which is always weaker than its adversary. For all their unmotivatedly evil dragons and all their unbelievably stalwart heroes and heroines, folktales are about us, about our lives in *this* world.

Cinderella, for instance, embodies the same truth as Our Lady's "Magnificat": "He has exalted the humble"—for no reason except that the humble are in need and for that very reason, to God, are lovable. *Beauty and the Beast* taken literally is impossible but taken figuratively is as undeniable as the multiplication tables: When someone ugly is loved, he or she becomes beautiful. *Jack and the Beanstalk* is a tale true for anyone, from little David to the rising young executive of today: if you want to climb high, if you want the goose that lays the golden eggs, be warned: you have to contend with giants. (See Bruno Bettelheim, *The Uses of Enchantment.)*

Rooted in the real. The most bizarre science fiction tale is based on scientific data we have now and on human beings as we know them. The most enchanted fairy castle also has its foundations in real life. Like the story of Youth, it may be two steps removed from a photographic reality, but the very removal helps us see our ordinary lives in a new perspective.

No children (much less beagles!) speak with such sophistication as the *Peanuts* crew and Snoopy, just as no boy's head is as round as Charlie Brown's. But the very distortion of the pictures and adult reactions from the mouths of children make us see our own lives more clearly—because of the distortion.

The Big "IF." Besides whatever specific truths any folk story might convey under its surface enchantments, every one is based on what Chesterton called "the doctrine of conditional joy": All joy and all success hangs by an "if" in a folktale—and in life. "You can win the beautiful princess and live happily ever after *if* you can go through a wall of nettles without saying, 'Ouch!'" Or, "The palace of sapphire and gold is yours *if* you can chop off the heads of fifty ferocious dragons."

This, really, is the law of life: You can really enjoy martinis *if* you don't guzzle five at once; you can really enjoy material goods *if* you don't become enslaved to them. And the message of Christianity is exactly the same as the message of folktales: You will find your full life *if* you are willing to forget yourself and risk that life.

Parables Again

Parables are not restricted to the gospels. Franz Kafka wrote stories which, like the ones in the gospels, are really riddles about the condition of humans in the universe. He could have written literal articles in learned journals about the way modern society dehumanizes us. Instead, he wrote a story called "Metamorphosis" in which a young man named Gregor Samsa gradually turns into a big cockroach. In *The Trial*, a man is accused of a crime which is nameless; he is tried and condemned, and to the very end, he never knows what he's done. It is a parable about our feelings of formless guilt from no apparent cause.

Such stories bring to the surface our subconscious fears and make them solid, concrete, so we can examine them more clearly. A similar fear called "the actor's dream" is a nightmare, which seems almost universal among actors, that they are onstage and not only have they forgotten their lines, but they can't even remember what the play is about! Dreams themselves are parables that our subconscious tells us all during the night.

Another parable, as old as Aesop, is Plato's parable of the cave. Figuratively, Plato is talking about a cave. What is he really talking about?

"Take the following parable about ignorance and education as a picture of our nature. Imagine humankind dwelling in a cave with a long entrance tunnel open to the light from the cave opening. They have been there since childhood, with necks and legs chained so they sit looking only in one direction, toward the wall in front. But light comes from a fire burning behind them. Between the fire and the prisoners, imagine a low wall like the screens puppeteers hide behind while they are working unseen.

Along the pathway between that wall and the fire, bearers move carrying cutouts and statues of humans and animals and trees. Some bearers are talking, and some make noises like the noises of the imitations they carry. But all the prisoners can see are the shadows of the objects on the wall in front of them.

Suppose the prisoners are allowed to talk. Don't you think when they named the shadows they saw parading along the wall they would think they were seeing and naming the real things? If so, such prisoners would certainly believe there were no realities (other than themselves) except those shadows of imitations of real things, and the voices were the voices of the shadows.

Suppose now someone should drag one of the prisoners out of the cave by force, into the light of the sun. Wouldn't he be terrified and furious at being hauled out of security? And when he came into the light, it would blind him, and at first he wouldn't be able to see the things that are really real.

He thinks back to the place he lived his cramped life, what passed for wisdom in that place, and his benighted fellow prisoners. Don't you think he would feel fortunate and pity the people he left behind? He would rather take anything than live like that again.

Then picture him going back and sitting in his old seat. Now his eyes are full of darkness, coming out of the sun. If he were to tell those people the real truth, the difference between reality and shadows, wouldn't they laugh him to scorn? Wouldn't they say his eyesight has been ruined by leaving the cave? And wouldn't they kill anyone who tried to release them and take them outside?"

This is a parable every teacher would find full of resonances: despite the fact that it is "made up," written 2,500 years ago, what insights does it give us about the relation between watching television and the real world?

Reflection

Just as Plato did, Jesus used parables as a teaching tool, because they were clearer and more appealing than academic lecturing and far easier to remember. In his parable of the wedding feast, Matthew sums up the whole history of salvation. Whom do you think he really means beneath the figurative symbols of: the king, the prince, the invited guests and "their town," the servants (especially the third group), the feast itself, and that puzzling guest at the end. And what is his "wedding garment"? (He is talking to Jews unwilling to accept him.)

"The kingdom of heaven may be compared to a king who gave a feast for his son's wedding. He sent his servants to call those who had been invited, but they would not come. Next he sent more servants. 'Tell those who have been invited,' he said, 'that I have my banquet prepared, my oxen and fattened cattle have been slaughtered, everything is ready. Come to the wedding.' But they were not interested: one went off to his farm, another to his business, and the rest seized his servants, maltreated them and killed them.

"The king was furious. He despatched his troops, destroyed those murderers and burnt their town. Then he said to his servants, 'The wedding is ready, but as those who were invited proved to be unworthy, go to the crossroads in the town and invite everyone you can find to the wedding.'

"So the servants went out onto the roads and collected together everyone they could find, bad and good alike; and the wedding hall was filled with guests.

"When the king came in to look at the guests he noticed one man who was not wearing a wedding garment, and said to him, 'How did you get in here, my friend, without a wedding garment?' And the man was silent.

"Then the king said to the attendants, 'Bind him hand and foot and throw him out into the dark, where there will be weeping and grinding of teeth.' For many are called, but few are chosen."

(Matthew 22:2–14)

Part Three

How The Gospel Became The Gospels

Chapter Six

HISTORICAL/HISTORIC

Jesus didn't write the gospels. The first Christian communities did. Strangely, many good Christians are rather surprised when they realize that the church came before the gospels. Of course they realize that Jesus didn't write things like "And then Jesus said," but they are shocked, even scandalized, when some seeming apostate suggests that even every word quoted by the evangelists as coming from Jesus' mouth is not necessarily a perfectly accurate quotation. Somehow they would like to believe that someone in the backhills of first-century Palestine had a secret tape recorder and took everything down. If this were so, how would they explain the following quotations as "recorded" by three evangelists:

MATTHEW 24:19–20	*MARK 13:11*	*LUKE 21:14–15*
When they deliver you up do not be anxious how you are to speak or what you are to say; for what you are to say will be given to you in that hour; for it is not you who speak, but the Spirit of your Father speaking through you.	And when they bring you to trial and deliver you up, do not be anxious beforehand what you are to say; but say whatever is given you in that hour for it is not you who speak but the Holy Spirit.	Settle it therefore in your minds, not to meditate beforehand how to answer; for I will give you a mouth and wisdom, which none of your adversaries will be able to withstand or contradict.

Although each of the quotations says substantially the same thing, which one is the statement of the real Jesus? The absolutely accurate words? When people of simple faith encounter such a question—and this one is relatively uncomplicated compared to some of the differences in reportage we will see later—they are not merely confused, but their faith is terribly shaken, not just in the church or the gospels, but in Jesus himself. They might say, "If we don't have the absolutely accurate words of Jesus, then maybe the whole thing is a hoax! Maybe the whole thing is just 'made-up'!"

I am completely convinced that the whole thing was not just "made-up" or a hoax, but I am also convinced that the gospels are not absolutely accurate reportage of historical events, written at the very moment they occurred, like a modern TV news program. They were never intended to be. They were recording a myth—a way of telling the truth when the truth is too big for words.

No one can self-consciously invent a myth out of his or her head—not in the sense we have been using that word. It must be rooted in the real. It must arise out of the consciousness of a people and correspond to the-way-things-are as those people see things. In this sense, myth is meant to express their fundamental understandings of themselves and life. If the myth does that, it is true and valid and effective; if it doesn't, it just dies. The myth of atoms, for instance, describes a reality which can't be seen but whose effects can be seen. When we act as if the atom really looked like the Niels Bohr model, it works—even though no physicist would say that the model is an even remotely accurate picture of what an atom really looks like. Similarly, when we act as if the myth of progress were literally true—that anyone can be President if one works hard enough, that things are all getting better—a lot of things actually do get better.

In the same way, the central figure of the New Testament myth was a historical figure: a man who, we know from testimony, preached, healed, made certain claims about himself, was executed by a Roman official whose name we know, and returned to life in a way that convinced his followers. We have testimony to his historical existence from non-Christian writers, e.g., Josephus,

Pliny, Tacitus, Suetonius. In fact, we know he existed just as we know Socrates existed, and on the same kind of evidence. But we also know that over the course of 2,000 years this man's life and ideas have enriched the lives of countless millions of human beings. Even flawed, the myth validates itself in living it out.

There is a crucial distinction Laurence Perrin makes between "historical" and "historic." "Historical" means the actual event, what happened; "historic" means the event-as-interpreted: what it means in the whole perspective of human life and human significance. For instance, during the Civil War a great many men fought and died at Gettysburg, Pennsylvania. There was actual gunfire; certain men stood on certain spots; particular individuals died here and there. It was historical; it actually happened. But the event was just one more battle, just one more occurrence, until Abraham Lincoln interpreted it, put it into the whole perspective of what the war was all about and what human liberty is all about. As Mabel Lang has said, "In a very real sense, the chief reason that we remember what men did at Gettysburg is what Lincoln said there." The historical event became historic when Lincoln showed its meaning.

The death of Jesus was historical; it actually happened. But without the gospels, without interpretation, without someone to bring out its significance, it would be just one more man who died unjustly on a Roman cross. Facts and historical data are not enough. We listen to historical data on the TV news every night: L.A. is torn by riots, such-and-such company is raising prices, this or that product may cause cancer. But what does it all mean? Where does it all fit? So a commentator or a panel comes on and tries to tell us. St. Paul and the evangelists tried to do exactly the same thing.

The gospels are not a biography; they are a message, an interpretation of events. Granted the historical, biographical details about what Jesus did, what do they mean to us? The gospel was a historic message which Paul could proclaim in a single sentence:

> "First and foremost, I handed on to you the facts which had been imparted to me: that Christ died for our sins, in accordance with the scriptures; that he was buried; that he was raised to life on the third day, according to the scriptures; and that he appeared to Cephas, and afterwards to the Twelve. . .and in the end, he appeared even to me."   (1 Corinthians 15:3–8)

Facts are not enough for understanding; they have to be interpreted, put into the full context of our present lives. In a sense, every priest or deacon does this every Sunday when an event from scripture is read. He tries, with his own talents and limitations, to explain what the event means to his audience. In interpreting an event, one must explain who this person is, what he or she said and did, but one must also show the importance of this event beyond its mere occurrence: how this event should indeed change minds, change lives, change the whole course of history. Therefore, the evangelists spoke of the "historical" Jesus as he actually was but also of the "historic" Jesus as he was interpreted, his significance for future generations. And the authenticity of their interpretation is guaranteed by the inspiration of the Spirit of Jesus, still living in their midst.

Therefore, the New Testament myth—again, in the sense we have been using that word—is built around actual concrete, historical persons. But the myth, the message of the gospels, is proved not by whether Jesus actually did this or that miracle as it is described, or by whether he actually said these particular words in this particular order. It is validated by whether the message works when incorporated into life, whether the all-out Christian's life is enriched by the message. The core assertion of the gospel is that Jesus is the quintessence of both divinity and humanity, sent to announce and inaugurate the Kingdom, the unconditional love of our Father for those with no hope of salvation by Jewish standards. He is the revelation of God, God's Word, and the "best of us," and by living his life one can find joy.

Even as sophisticated a writer as the author of Luke-Acts could write about both the historical and the mythic in exactly the same way. The evangelist can distort historical events (as probably with the fantastic occurrences at the Crucifixion); he can even invent them (as probably with the Magi). The test of their validity is whether they legitimately extend the truth of the myth. As Perrin says, "The birth of Jesus did change forever the possibilities for a man living in the world; his ascension is a way of saying that there is now a futurity for human existence . . . that was not there before. The myth is a vividly pictorial way of interpreting the history."

The gospel writers use narrative to interpret events. For instance, Matthew lifts details out of Psalms 69 and 22, which were concerned with the righteous sufferer and God's vindication of him, and inserts them into his the events at Calvary.

MATTHEW 27
They offered him wine to drink, mingled with gall; but when he tasted it, he would not drink it. (v. 34)

And when they crucified him, they divided his garments among them by casting lots. . . . (v. 35)

And those who passed by derided him, wagging their heads and saying, "You who would destroy the temple

PSALMS
They gave me poison to eat instead; when I was thirsty they gave me vinegar to drink. (69:21)

They divide my garments among them and cast lots for my clothes. (22:18)

All who see me jeer at me, they toss their heads and sneer. (22:7)

and build it in three days, save
yourself! If you are the Son of God
come down from the cross. . . ."
(v. 39)

"He trusts in God; let God deliver   "He relied on Yahweh, let Yahweh
him now, if he desires him; for he   save him! If Yahweh is his friend, let
said, 'I am the Son of God.' " (v. 43)   Him rescue him!" (22:8)

What does it matter if some loathsome little sadist actually, historically, did or did not blaspheme with his own scriptures over a dying man? These narrative details may or may not be true at the level of factual history, but they are included because *ipso facto* they put the crucifixion of Jesus into its truest context: Jesus *is* the righteous sufferer whom God vindicated, and therefore is the fulfillment of Psalms 69 and 22. Moreover, the Jesus-event looks not only backward to the psalms but forward to the present (when the evangelist was writing) when dedicated Christians were living out not only the life of Jesus but his sufferings as well.

Therefore, the New Testament is history, both *historical and historic,* i.e., the historical interpreted by means of myth: narration, hyperbole, irony—the whole treasury of figurative communication. It is a method which narrates the events in such a way that the narration itself (even if details are invented) is a commentary and an interpretation of the historical events. Therefore, if one of the evangelists diverges from the others in his choice of words, or changes the audience or setting in which the same speech is given, or puts a particular event in a different place in his overall narrative from the others, the choice is motivated by his conviction that some nuance or facet of the basic message will be better served by his placement—whether or not this event historically occurred here or there.

Some events of the gospels are actually historical (like the crucifixion of Jesus), some are mythic (like Matthew's addition of earthquakes and yawning graves at Jesus' death), some are merely legendary (like the angels at Bethlehem), but the *whole complex is historic.* Just because one's attempts to capture the uncapturable are inadequate does not mean those attempts are bad—or that the uncapturable reality doesn't exist. The gospels are, in a sense, sermons—designed to elicit in the reader a faith-response to the core truth that they propose and thereby to enrich his or her life. As Perrin writes:

> "The parables of Jesus were remembered and handed on as tradition within the Christian communities, but as they were handed on they were reinterpreted both by changes within the texts of the parables themselves and also by the addition of new conclusions or explanations to them. Then, when the evangelists incorporated them into their gospels, they introduced further changes to make them express the meaning they saw in them. . . . A fundamental aspect of the New Testament texts is that they are in no small part the end product of a long and constant process of interpretation and reinterpretation."

Just as Peter, in his homily on Pentecost, felt free to reinterpret the prophet Joel, so the author of Luke-Acts did a little reinterpreting of his own of Peter's reinterpretation. And any priest who composes a homily on that passage in Acts does a little more reinterpreting himself. The criterion of truth is whether the homily really speaks of the way things really are—not merely as one individual sees them, but as God sees things. It is, like the work of the prophets, interpreting the historical in the name of God.

Similarly, once the early church had the gospel of Mark, why did they bother writing three more? There is no essential change in the *core* statement of Mark when the reader moves to Matthew and Luke and John. But each of the evangelists, as we shall see later in more detail, took the historical facts and the interpretations made before him and saw different shadings, different insights into what Jesus said and did which would help his audience. And there is a time lapse between the gospel versions; more data had come to light, too good not to be included.

For instance, Mark was probably written for non-Palestinian Christians, former pagans, probably Romans. He explicitly translates Aramaic words into Greek for them; he has less concern than the others to connect the message of Jesus with the Old Testament; he underscores the meaning of the gospel for newly baptized pagans, especially those who suffer persecution for their faith.

From similar evidence, we can legitimately infer Matthew was written for Jewish converts. His central purpose seems to be to show conclusively that Jesus is the Messiah Jews hoped for. His division into five books parallels the five books of the Jewish law. He quotes the Old Testament as evidence that Jesus is the new Moses and the Christian community is the new Israel.

Luke, the most literary of the gospels, seems by the elegance of its Greek to be directed at a more learned audience, and it is, indeed, explicitly addressed to a prominent man named Theophilus—both the gospel of Luke and the book of Acts. Luke's reassessment of the gospel message could well have been motivated at least in part by his attempt to understand why the expected Second Coming had not occurred, since he softpedals references to its nearness and emphasizes that its time is quite indefinite. He writes primarily for Gentiles and therefore never uses the Aramaic words common in Matthew, like "rabbi" or "Abba" or "hosanna." Instead he calls Jesus "Teacher" or

"Master." As is obvious from his addition of parables which the others do not seem to have known about, he was concerned about interpreting the message of Jesus about the poor, outcasts, women, and Gentiles.

The version by John, from the style of the Greek, seems to have been written in large part by an author or authors more used to thinking in Aramaic. John has no parables, no simple moral instructions, no debates about the Law with Jewish officials. Instead, we have much allegory and involved symbolism, which leads scholars to believe the author was trying to translate the message into terms understood by those familiar with current Greek religious and philosophical ideas and language. It is, then, the reflection on the message by a theologian with a strong philosophical, symbolic, even mystical interest.

When each successive evangelist began his work, he did not set out to "correct" the original Mark. Apparently, each thought that the gospel versions as he knew them failed to render Jesus fully, in a way easily comprehensible to his own particular audience. For this reason, he used some new material he had discovered in the traditions of his own community and reworked the old. Like four different artists painting the same subject, each gives us a unique insight into one and the same Jesus. It would be quibbling to say that their reinterpretations of their common material was illegitimate.

As an exercise, focus on a living or recently deceased person whom you admire. Research all you can in libraries; write letters to people who knew that person until you have at least five replies. Then write a life of that person. You'll have done exactly what the evangelists did about Jesus.

Why So Late?

When I first began to study theology and scripture, it was a great strain on my faith when I learned that reputable scripture scholars put the date of Mark, the earliest gospel version, somewhere between 60–70 A.D.—about thirty years after the events it describes. That gap made me nervous. Why did they wait so long? A lot of distortion can creep into mouth-to-ear chains of communication; Why hadn't they "locked up" the definitive version as soon as possible after it actually, historically happened?

There were several reasons the gospel message was passed along orally rather than in written form. First, early Christians were not very "literary" people; many were probably illiterate. Education was confined mostly to the wealthy and aristocratic, and at first, there was no value in writing everything down when there were so few converts who could read it.

Second, and more important, such people were far more willing to accept testimony when it was delivered face-to-face. Moreover, the early audience for the gospel had an extraordinary training in memory devices—which is one reason scholars suspect that the core of the beatitudes (which depend on a formula) and the parables (which have a story form) are the closest we have to accurate recollections of Jesus' actual words. Such people were not distracted as we are by the glut of television, newspapers, magazines, and billboards. They had a small—and therefore easily learned—body of literature which was their whole library of religion, culture, and entertainment. When you have nothing else to do in your spare time, whether you spend it whittling or retelling stories, you tend to become very good at it.

The most important reason for the delay in writing it all down was the fact that most early Christians believed the end of the world was at hand. It hardly seems profitable to write history when you believe history is about to end. Paul wrote letters—the earliest parts of the New Testament—not because he hoped they would be preserved for many generations but because he was doing exactly the work of the gospel—interpreting the message of Jesus to particular audiences and their particular problems at the moment. His interpretations were written simply because he was in one place and his audiences were in other places. He would far rather have handled the interpretations orally, but that was impossible. Paul probably never even dreamed he was writing "scripture."

Most likely, many of the oral communications about the life and words of Jesus were put together in small written collections centered around a common theme: poverty and riches, seed parables, various beatitudes—all statements which various witnesses recalled Jesus making, brought together in little scrolls—even though Jesus may have spoken them on many different occasions. These were for the convenience of preachers and catechists. Finally, Mark collected such booklets, combined them and arranged them into a "full" treatment of the life and message of Jesus.

There were three critical reasons such overall treatments were finally needed. First, the validity of the message depended on the eyewitnesses present when it was given and lived. The first disciples were the foundation of the church. But when they began to die, their witness had to be concentrated into documents to validate what was said about Jesus.

Second, the early Christian community was dominated by the belief that the end was at hand. When that event just didn't happen, the community had to sit down and reexamine, to reassess their overliteral interpretation of what Jesus had revealed of God's plan. They believed utterly that the new order had come in Jesus, but they were faced with the equally undeniable evidence that the old order had not yet passed away. They began to see that it would be a matter of time before the new Kingdom would be fulfilled and that most of them would live full lives and die before the Second Coming occurred. Therefore, the focus of their reinterpretations of the message had to shift from preparing for the immediate end to history and settle on understanding how the message should be applied to an ordinary life.

Third, there was just the natural inclination to reflect on and probe more deeply into the meaning of the person and message of the most important Person in human history. If the message is "Jesus is Lord," then what is he like? In what concrete ways can I, in a different place and time, be like him? If Jesus fulfills all the expectations of Hebrew scripture, how? These are questions the written gospels were meant to begin answering.

Finally, as the church began to spread in the Greco-Roman world, interpretation of the gospel message became subject to influence by all kinds of foreign religious and philosophic movements. Thus, it was in danger of being adapted and reinterpreted in ways different from—or even contrary to—Jesus' original intention and the experience of the first apostolic witnesses. It was necessary to assure that its basic message was rooted in the life and ideas of the historically real Jesus. In a sense, the church does the same thing even today, testing each new adaptation against the recorded intentions of its founder.

Faith

The gospels, then, are a collection of things Jesus actually, historically did say and do. But they also contain some events and sayings which the early Christian community made up and "had" Jesus do and say—to demonstrate how Jesus would have acted, *consistent with his basic historical message,* in situations he did not in fact encounter but which troubled the people who came after him. They were also dotted with pious legends which, though historically "untrue," nonetheless were used as vehicles to fill out other facets of the message (as the Magi were). As Christians, we believe that the Spirit guided the church to understand and describe the person and mission of Jesus in terms that Jesus himself may never have known or used.

But doesn't this raise a credibility problem? Who knows which is which? Even then someone may ask, "Who is this person to tell me what Jesus *would* have said if such-and-such problem had come up?"

In answer to the first point, there are men and women who can give a pretty good idea which elements of the gospels are most likely completely historical, which are extensions of the message to later problems and the reasons why this extension was done, and which are legends and what facet of the message they were intended to fill out. Their answers are found in commentaries on scripture, like the enormously detailed but very readable *Jerome Biblical Commentary.* Any serious reader of the scriptures can find the level of any saying or event of the Bible—from Genesis to Revelation—in one of the commentaries. Although scholars may disagree, although they almost always hedge with words like "more than likely," they are scrupulously honest.

The answer to the "who is this person" question is more difficult, since the attitude it betrays at least suggests that, like Thomas, the objector is not going to be convinced unless he or she puts physical fingers into Jesus' physical wounds. As John says in the only beatitude in his gospel: "Blessed are those who have not seen and yet believe." Only the person who has really *lived* the gospel can really read the gospels. A myth is, after all, validated only when a person lives it out and finds it actually works, actually enriches his or her life.

The Christian believer is not the naive simpleton many non-believers would like to picture. Surely Aquinas and Thomas More and John XXIII are evidence of that. One needs only to read a few pages of Teilhard de Chardin or Bernard Lonergan to find that brilliant people have believed and passionately so. But "despite" their brilliance, they are willing to accept the life and death of this Jesus as having cosmic implications in their own lives. They are willing because they have lived the message fully and found in the living a joy other people did not have.

The message of the myth has been even further verified by their profound experiences of the living God in prayer. Their gospel-enriched lives and their encounter with God proved beyond proof that the evangelists who reinterpreted and fabricated had every right to do so—since their embellishments are absolutely consistent with the basic message of Jesus and their own experience of God. If the words of Jesus were inspired by the Spirit within him, the words of the early Christian community were inspired in their turn by that same Spirit.

When I was wrestling with this crisis of faith myself in my first year of theological studies, I remember that the only thing that kept me going for a long while was the fact that my two scripture professors still said Mass every morning. With unaccustomed wisdom I said to myself, "Those two men know more loopholes and problems about the scriptures than I'll ever know, but they still say Mass. There must be an answer I just haven't found." And there was: living it and praying it.

Think of the gospel metaphor we decompacted earlier in these pages: "Finding the Kingdom of God is like finding a treasure in your field." The difference between the non-believer and the believer—or between those who have only been baptized and those who have actually been converted—is that true believers, the converted, feel a thrill of understanding about being Christians which the others have yet to comprehend.

The non-believer is usually someone who has not had that experience of God indisputably communicating to him or her. If it had been communicated, such a person would obviously have become a believer! Such a man or woman can read the Bible as the record of an ancient people—filled with myths, poems, fictional narratives, legal papers, advice, etc.—just as he or she would read the collected monuments of the Egyptians or Bantus and Mayans. It is a fascinating academic study. But only the believer can find the intended meaning.

The man or woman of faith—the fully convinced believer—is more like one who has "been to the mountain and seen." The believer is not always so sure what he or she has seen, but believers are sure they have seen something. The believer has had an experience of an encounter with a personal force which blew his or her mind. It was more real than any communication with another, more exhilarating than any daydream, more startling than merely being "struck by an idea." Such prayerful men and women believe that the active presence of God is working in this structure of myths. They believe that the same Person who speaks to them in this strange and incommunicable way also speaks through the words and events and symbols of the scriptures. For the non-believer, reading the scripture is like eavesdropping on a conversation between friends. For the believer, it is like being in on the conversation as one of the friends.

If you haven't had this realization, if you haven't had the mind-blowing experience of seeing it all fall together, you will just have to take the word of those who have.

Finding the Intended Meaning

The gospels are not unbiased. They were written by men of faith for men and women of faith. Trying to describe the difference in the impact of reading the scriptures after one believes—as opposed to reading them before one believed—is like trying to explain winning an Olympic medal to a couch potato. One has to get into the disciples' shoes and walk around in them to duplicate, even remotely, the enormity of what they intended to say and what their faith-filled audience heard.

To find the correct interpretation of a scripture passage means to find the interpretation that God and the author intended. The author, like the prophets, was interpreting events in the light of the mind of God, as manifested throughout history in God's dealings with men and women. Therefore, when reading scripture, one must search for two intended meanings: the intended meaning of the author for his time and place, and the intended meaning of God for all times and places.

Before taking each of these in turn, remember the distinction we saw before between "I worked my hands to the bone for you" and "I worked very hard for you." The intended meaning is neither the stripped-down, demythologized, bare literal meaning, nor is it a purely figurative meaning over which the imagination can run wild. It is something in between. At the one extreme, the purely academic scripture scholar can get to the literal meaning, whether he or she believes Jesus is Lord or not. At the other extreme, the wild-eyed enthusiast can wax poetic and draw all kinds of figurative conclusions light-years away from what the writer intended ("Even the devil can quote scripture to prove a point"; "My opinion's as good as anybody else's!"). But only the mind and heart and spirit of the balanced believer can penetrate to what the author and his Inspirer really meant.

What the Gospel Author Intended

To find out what a passage of scripture meant when it was written, one has to look at two things: (1) the literary form of the passage and (2) the meaning of the passage in the particular author's overall plan.

The first question is the literary form. Is the author at this point speaking literally or figuratively? For instance, if he refers to Jerusalem, does he mean it as the actual city or as a symbol for the church (the new Israel) or for heaven (the City of God)? Or all three? When you know that in the Book of Daniel, say, the author is secretly writing a series of short stories about a contemporary king and not recording the actual history of a long-dead one, you begin to understand that he didn't necessarily claim to have seen four beasts with eyes and wings all over them. You begin to realize that the authors of the New Testament are not to be judged by the criteria of strict historical method but by the criteria of truthful preaching and teaching. If one admits that a certain part of the scripture is fiction, he or she is not denying its historicity—because it was never meant to be historical. Biblical fiction is just as inspired and just as true as biblical history. We will see this later when we consider *form criticism*.

The second question is the place of this section in the author's overall plan. There is a special problem in biblical study because of the long history of editing, interpreting, and reinterpreting pieces of material over and over again. What has this author done to the material handed on to him? As we have seen, the books of the New Testament were the result of a *process*: they were not written by one man but by a whole series of people, and each was inspired to see some different facet as he reworked the material and passed it on.

When Mark wrote to his Roman pagan converts and Matthew wrote to his Jewish converts, they had two very different audiences. The two men had the same basic intention and message, but the parts of their gospels—even those dealing with the same event—are given a different coloration because of the differing interests and receptivities of their audiences. As we will see when comparing the same events in Mark, Matthew, and Luke, the individual author's theological intention in each passage comes clear in the way he adapts material common to all three. We will see this later when we consider *redaction (editorial) criticism.*

(1) Therefore, to find the author's intended meaning, one must first see what literary form he uses to get this idea across (*form criticism*) and then (2) how this particular event has been adapted and edited by this particular author (*redaction* [editorial] *criticism*). For answers to these two questions on any particular passage of the Bible, one can look in the *Jerome Biblical Commentary* or any similar work.

What God Intended

Each individual writer in the scriptures was writing to his own people, at a particular time, about particular problems. But his writing also fits into the whole overall sweep and perspective of the two Testaments—the whole historic pattern of God's relationship with people. This author's communication has a particular meaning at a particular time, but seen against this longer perspective of God's consistent pattern of fidelity, what the author says takes on an even richer meaning. When Isaiah saw Israel as the suffering servant of God, he did not see a young carpenter-rabbi hauling his cross up to Calvary. What he saw was his people suffering for their faith, and he urged them to see that Yahweh had always rewarded that faith. But, seen in the whole history of God's dealings with the faithful, including dealings through Jesus with the New Israel, Isaiah's vision has even deeper meanings than Isaiah himself could have known.

How can a writer write a work which has meanings even he or she doesn't know? Let me give an example. When I wrote a musical called "Tender Is the Knight," I intended it to be a satire on education, on people being trained to combat the ideas of people they have never even met. The knights trained to kill dragons and the dragons trained to kill knights sheerly on the basis of propaganda, without ever asking themselves whether they really wanted to kill their so-called opposition or even whether the opposition deserved to be killed. I had intended it to be a gentle poke at my own theological training and was half-tempted to call the dragons names like "Luther" and "Calvin." But when the show was over, people were asking me if it was a satire on war. Others wondered if it were a satire on racial prejudice. I hadn't been thinking of those idiocies when I wrote it, but I had to admit—after the fact—that what I had said was true of those human activities as well as of any kind of witless antagonism based on uncritical use of propaganda. Similarly, later members of the church could see implications in the gospels that the original writers may not have purposely put there.

What, then, are the criteria by which a reader can tell that he or she has more or less gotten the meaning God intended—over and above the intentions of the individual writer?

First of all, this larger sense has to be a legitimate development of the author's intended meaning—as it was with the further insights into "Tender Is the Knight." It must be a fuller understanding of the original and not merely a wrenching of the original. When modern fundamentalists see the Antichrist in the book of Revelation as a foreshadowing of Hitler or Napoleon or the Roman papacy, they are seeing something far different from the writer's intention. When St. Augustine turns the parable of the Good Samaritan into an allegory of the fall of man, he is wrenching the author's text far from the author's intention. But when a modern preacher sees today's widespread paganism and materialism as a parallel to Israel's whoring after idols, or when he sees the starving of the world as the man beaten by the roadside and the capitalist nations as the priest and levite, he is legitimately applying the author's meaning to a situation the author could never have envisioned. In this way, the scripture truly is God's Word for all time, even though it was written by men of the first century for men and women of the first century.

Secondly, it is wise to know something about the whole Bible to be sure that the wider meaning one sees actually is a part of a continuing pattern of God's dealings with people. The New Testament writers, inspired by God, see that just as God fed the Israelites with manna, he feeds the New Israel with the Eucharist. What Moses was to Israel, Jesus was to the Christian church. What Jesus says implicitly becomes explicit when Paul and Acts interpret Jesus' acts and words. Still later, the church reflects on the scriptures and evolves even more out of them in the light of ever-expanding human knowledge.

These two criteria aren't always easy to apply, and it's worth being cautious before one stands up and says he or she has a totally new insight into a passage. Those whose knowledge of the Bible is vastly superior to yours or mine are far more hesitant and more willing to submit their theories to the judgment and authority of their peers.

What Is the Meaning for Me?

One can get to the author's intended meaning at least on the literary level, and know what every scholar in the world has to say about a particular passage, and know how this notion has been treated throughout the whole course of scripture—without his or her life being changed. For them, studying the Bible is no different from studying the sources and techniques and dates of Shakespeare's plays. If the Bible is no more than "exam fodder" or a source of proof-texts for debate, one's religious convictions and spiritual life will remain unaffected.

In reading scripture, as in reading Shakespeare, there is a place for both head and heart. One can analyze, dissect, probe logical relationships as a mathematician would—and the text will yield up far more than it ever has before. But, analysis done, one must go back and reread the text with completely different powers of the soul—imagination, emotion, love, spirit—not as a critic would but as a poet would. Otherwise, one is left after the analysis with the various parts of a corpse. Analysis reveals hidden parts, but only imagination can reenliven them.

One can study *Hamlet* line by line, word by word, but the only purpose of that careful analysis is so that the next time one sees the actual play it will echo even more broadly and profoundly in one's soul. Similarly, one can analyze the gospels line by line, word by word, but the only purpose of that analysis is so that the next time one prayerfully rereads that passage, the risen Jesus shines through the lines even more powerfully and with finer resonances. Both the mathematician and the poet are needed; one without the other is insufficient. Neither the dry demythologizing of the critic nor the wild rhapsodizings of the fanatic will put one in authentic contact with the living Christ.

A purely objective observer of the sayings and events of scripture—whether he or she was actually there or whether he or she reads about them 2,000 years later—will never truly find the intended meaning of those books until they are read with the eyes of a believer. The gospels are written from a faith rooted deeply in people's experience of the eternal. Surely, one can get a general idea of what's being said in them if he or she knows the "literary codes." But one will never reexperience them as they were intended and as they were first read until undergoing oneself that same experience of the eternal. When you meet the hero of the gospels for yourself, person-to-Person, the gospels become whole new books.

But how do we get those who have not met this hero to risk praying? Perhaps we can only tantalize them by the joy of our lives.

Chapter Seven

THE SEEDBED: DEVELOPMENT OF CHRISTIAN THOUGHT

The gospels are unexplainable unless one considers the religious movement, the early Christian community, which gave them birth. The gospels are not so much a historical outline as a record of the development of Christian thought. The content of what became solidified in the New Testament was generated by an evolving community, trying to apply the message of Jesus to new situations, trying to explicitate what Jesus had declared only implicitly, trying to defend itself against attack by Jews and Gentiles. The evolution described in this chapter is not as hard-and-fast as the section headings would suggest. All the stages existed alongside one another and influenced one another. But it is helpful to see the variety of influences that the early community underwent on its way from Jerusalem to Rome, from a sect within Judaism to an independent religion with a worldwide mission. Further, since Paul did not put dates on his letters, and since the early church was not interested in accurate dates and places, the dates given must always be taken as approximate. However, if the gospels are a product of an evolutionary process, it is helpful to see even a sketchy picture of that development.

The First Years:
Jewish Christians in Palestine

The first Christians were Jews. And they were still Jews not merely as citizens but in their religious lives as well. For a long time, against Paul's resistance, Peter believed that, equivalently, a Gentile had to become a Jew before he or she became Christian: males to be circumcised, all to observe the Jewish dietary laws. They still attended services in the Temple and still kept all the details of the Jewish law, even after the resurrection. They were a sect of Judaism, just like the Pharisees, Sadducees, Essenes, Zealots. They believed in the same Yahweh and the same scriptures. The only difference between them and their Jewish brethren was that they claimed Jesus was the Messiah and that this claim had been validated by the resurrection. This, in turn, was a direct attack on the privileged place of the Law and the Temple. But that was more than enough to make them hounded apostates in the eyes of their fellow Jews.

Since we have no writings from those first twenty years except what was incorporated into later works like the gospels, we can only speculate from the linguistic "layers" and varying styles of the New Testament what the particular interests of that first network of communities were. It seems that the community in Jerusalem itself was particularly conservative, legalistic, and accepted by its satellite communities as authoritative. This conservatism could have been motivated, at least in part, by the fact that Jerusalem was the focus of the Jewish religion and therefore the place where Christians were forced to explain themselves in terms the pharisaic mind could understand.

It is safe to suspect that they had at least two purposes in their initial development of the core gospel message: (1) to explain what the Good News meant to their reluctant neighbors and (2) to defend themselves when they were hauled before the "sanhedrins and synagogues." One persecutor, Saul of Tarsus, by his own admission stood by while Stephen, the first martyr, was stoned to death for his "heresies."

After the basic proclamation that the Kingdom had indeed begun, one of their first tasks was to explain to skeptical and hostile Jews why the expected Messiah suffered such a degrading death. To do so, they combed the Hebrew scriptures—which both orthodox Jews and Christians revered—to show how Jesus had been and still was the fulfillment of God's constant dealings with Israel as God's suffering servant. Also, they tried to explain the special table fellowship they had together in the community since the days of Jesus: the

Eucharist. Appealing to their common heritage, they argued that it was the fulfillment of the Passover supper wherein Jews celebrated their release from bondage in Egypt and their inauguration as the People of God. But the Christian meal was not celebrating their physical release from the Romans (as the Passover celebrated the physical release from the Egyptians); it celebrated their release, within themselves, from the values of the Kingdom of the World.

By scientific linguistic techniques, scholars can isolate within our present texts of the Greek New Testament forms and styles that go back to the very earliest days of the church. All scholars will agree that, deep below the additions by later writers, there is a body of statements traceable back to the very first years. For short, they call this sayings-source "Q" (from the German, *Quelle*, "Source"). Within a few years of the resurrection of Jesus, this was probably already written in a scroll or booklet. It contained, in no more than two hundred or so verses, sayings and stories of Jesus, preserved in Aramaic and only later translated into Greek. We will see more of "Q" in the next chapter, since its contents are threaded here and there throughout the gospel versions of Matthew and Luke (not Mark).

Isolating these earlier linguistic elements in our present gospels, scholars find that the general tone of the "Q" sayings and stories is dominated by a concern about the nearness of the End. Also, since the only potential converts at the moment were their fellow Jews, much of "Q" is concerned with explaining the meaning of the message of the Kingdom as it was connected with the Hebrew scriptures, showing that—like Isaiah, Jeremiah, and Daniel—Jesus was a prophet interpreting history in the name of God and that his prophetic Spirit lived on in the Christian community. According to F. C. Grant, this very early "gospel-before-the-gospels" contained more or less the following:

—The ministry and message of John the Baptizer

—The temptation of Jesus

—The Sermon on the Mount

—The mission of the twelve

—Jesus' teaching about prayer and the Our Father.

—Various controversies with the scribes and pharisees, especially the charge of relation to Beelzebub

—Jesus' teaching about discipleship:
freedom from care,
watchfulness,
the kingdom as a treasure

—Parables of the mustard seed and the yeast

—Sayings about the law and forgiveness

—Sayings about the Second Coming and the parable of the entrusted talents.

This list does not claim that "Q" contained these ideas in the *form* in which they are presently found in the gospels, but that, within a few years of the beginning, the seed was there.

The Mission to Jews Outside Palestine

The greatest developments in the message came when the early community took the Good News to the "outside world." And that world was *Hellenistic.*

"Hellenism" (from the Greek word *Hellas,* "Greece") is the name given to the civilization created and spread by the conquests of Alexander the Great (331–323 B.C.). As he conquered the whole known world, from the Greek peninsula to India and from North Africa to Persia, his men brought with them the ideas and customs and language of Greece. Everywhere Greek culture was imitated, and every people spoke Greek, even Palestinian Jews. The effect of this common language increased enormously the possibility of interchanging ideas, with the result that, while every culture became Hellenized, even Palestinian Judaism, each culture also gave its own coloration to Hellenism as it spread farther with the expansion of the new world empire, Rome.

The Roman conquest did not change the cultural situation very much, since Romans derived their culture from Greece. Only in the second century A.D. (100–199) did Latin spread eastward from the West and split the world into a Latin world centered in Rome and a Greek world centered in Byzantium.

Jews were scattered throughout this Hellenistic world which was rich with conflicting faiths and philosophies. These Jews were bilingual, thinking and speaking easily in both Greek and Aramaic. They translated their Hebrew scriptures into Greek (the Septuagint) and built synagogues in each city where they lived so that they could worship Yahweh, even though they could not worship God "properly" in the Temple at Jerusalem.

Palestinian Jews distrusted Hellenistic Jews because they often seemed to be adopting "foreign ways." Therefore, when a Hellenized Jew like Paul came back to Jerusalem, he was doubly distrusted, both by the Jewish authorities he had once served and by the conservative converted Christian Jews. On the other hand, it made Paul a providential agent to take the Good News outside the parochial confines of Palestine.

Outside Palestine, Hellenistic Jews made their own contributions to Hellenism besides being affected by it. Many Gentile pagans, upset by the numberless "gods" and the vices of their times, were attracted by the monotheism and moral code of

Judaism. Some were fully converted, accepting even circumcision late in life and the full Jewish dietary laws. Others, although eager to share the Judaic way of life and worship, were understandably not as eager for circumcision and the strictures of Jewish ritual law. These were sufficiently numerous that the Hellenistic Jews coined a name for them: "the God-fearers." As the Christian Jews like Paul emerged from Palestine to share the Good News with their Hellenistic Jewish brethren, they found fertile ground for the seed in these "God-fearers."

Christianity appealed to such people because they were not forced to be circumcised, while at the same time participating fully in all that Judaism had to offer—and more. The story of this missionary movement to spread the gospel from Palestine to the outside world was later written in the Acts of the Apostles. The speeches it records are typical examples of Christian preaching in synagogues, to "God-fearers," and on the streets of Greek cities around the Mediterranean. It was these preachers, familiar with the Septuagint (Greek) translation of "Yahweh" (*kurios,* "Lord"), who summed up their message in the single sentence: "Jesus is Lord [Yahweh among us]."

Gentile Christians

Just as God had prepared the Hebrews for the Good News by the evolving ideas given them by the prophets of the Old Testament, God also prepared the Gentiles outside Palestine by the evolving ideas of the Hellenic thinkers and philosophers— Socrates, Plato, Aristotle, the Stoics, the mystery cults. The Greeks thought more naturally of redemption from the world rather than transformation of the world. They thought more naturally of the immortality of the soul than of the resurrection of the body. But the idea of an other-worldly, heroic redeemer, the conflict between flesh and spirit, the pentecostal gifts of the

Spirit in Christianity were something they could understand very well. As the Christian community grew outward from Palestine, it was more and more toward these well-disposed Gentiles that the New Testament writers turned in their attempt to "translate" the message into terms and categories the non-Jewish mind could comprehend.

Moreover, the authors of the epistles and gospels took great pains to ensure that their pagan audiences did not think that Jesus was "just one more god" or that Christianity was just one more mystery cult from the East. Paul, for instance, is insistent in his letters to the Corinthians that they control their wild enthusiasm in such activities as speaking in tongues and the like, lest their faith deteriorate into pseudo-religious orgies. Mark in his gospel strongly argues against the assertion that Jesus is merely one more "divinized man," like Hercules, who had been raised as a reward for his labors to the level of a demigod because he found favor with the gods of Olympus. The Christian community was more than willing to be enriched by the new insights of Gentile converts, but it was strongly unwilling to be diluted by them.

As Christianity moved out into the Hellenistic world, which was more sophisticated and varied than the relatively simpler Palestinian culture, the different expectations and receptivities of this new audience called for adaptations of methods in preaching. Unlike the stories and sayings of the "Q" document which served the Palestinian communities, the letters of Paul to the missionary churches take the form of general Christian instruction—not stories and sayings of Jesus but theological reflections on the implications of the core Kingdom message. Whereas the early community had done this (and still continued to do it) by fabricating stories about Jesus to show how he would have applied the message to a later problem, Paul forthrightly proclaimed his interpretation with far fewer mythic devices. There is very little interest in Paul's letters about the story of the historical Jesus other than in accounts of the founding of the Eucharist, the passion, and the resurrection. These letters, which were sent originally to communities around the Mediterranean, were later copied and sent elsewhere to be read at eucharistic meetings, since they dealt with characteristic problems Christians faced everywhere in non-Jewish cultures: the relation of pagan Hellenistic forms of religious enthusiasm to the Christian's possession of the Spirit, the relation of the resurrection of Jesus to the future resurrection of the believer, and so on.

One problem for the beginning reader of scripture today is to get straight in his or her mind that, although the Acts of Apostles speaks of the history of the early church and especially of the missionary journeys of Paul, and although it is printed in most Bible versions before the epistles, it was written *after* the epistles had long been in circulation, and about twenty years after the events it describes. Moreover, it was written for an audience different from Paul's own, one which had had longer time to reflect and assimilate the original message. Therefore, if one wants to get some idea of the second and third phases of the church's evolving understanding—the mission to Jews outside Palestine and then to Gentiles, he or she can get a better idea from Paul's letters than from Acts.

It might help to understand this difference if we considered one event—the Council of Jerusalem—which is treated by both Paul and Acts. Paul discusses it in Galatians (2:1–10), which was written between 50 and 55 A.D. and the same event in Acts (15:1–19), which was written between 70 and 90 A.D. Paul was not only an earlier writer, he was also an eyewitness to the Council.

Paul describes the "Council" between himself and the leaders of the Jerusalem community (Peter, James, John) as resulting from his willingly coming to those eyewitness authorities to submit for their judgment the content of his preaching and his interpretation of the message. Titus, Paul's companion, had not been obliged to be circumcised, and several converted Pharisees at the meeting insisted that circumcision was essential for Gentile converts. "I was so determined to safeguard you (Galatians) the true meaning of the Good News, that I refused even out of deference to yield to such people for one moment" (2:5).

It was a critical moment, since the result could greatly jeopardize the non-Jewish mission. But Paul argued on grounds of the liberty from the Law that Christians enjoy in Christ Jesus, and Peter agreed. Peter would concentrate his efforts more heavily on the conversion of the circumcised (Jews), and Paul would concentrate his on the uncircumcised (Gentiles). It was only later, in Antioch, that Peter and Paul met again, and Paul upbraided Peter for discontinuing his practice of eating with pagans, since Peter was wrongly associating the requirements for being a Christian with the requirements for being a Jew.

This same meeting is also described in Acts, written a generation later for an audience with different problems. The episode falls by design in the middle of the book, because it is the turning point in Luke's story: when the apostolic college at Jerusalem officially recognizes evangelizing Gentiles. In this act, the church officially breaks out of its Jewish womb. As Luke presents it, the council treated *both* problems: circumcision and the dietary laws, stressing that the authoritative Jerusalem church itself decided it would lay no conditions on Gentile converts. In speeches which Luke consciously makes up and puts on the lips of the speakers, Peter as the first of the disciples settles the circumcision question, and James as the head of the Jerusalem community solves the dietary questions. No speech of Paul is recorded at all; there is no mention of Titus.

Whichever version is historical is not the question, though the account by Paul is surely more likely since (1) he was there and (2) he was reporting it relatively soon after its occurrence. The version in Acts could well be a grouping together of several or many meetings on these same subjects, dramatically compacted here, complete with speeches to underscore its importance. The difference is a difference of purpose. Paul is using the event as a historical proof that the whole church agrees not to force Gentiles to accept Jewish customs. Luke is using the event on a more symbolic level to show that the focus of Christian concern is not on the Holy Land or the Holy City anymore but on the evangelization of the whole world. No preconceived limits should be set to that work. It must be remembered, too, that Paul wrote before the destruction of Jerusalem in 70 A.D. and Luke wrote after it. And that cataclysmic event more or less removed Palestinian Christianity from the scene as the central community.

The Jews revolted against Rome in 66 A.D., beginning a war they hoped Yahweh would help them win. When the war ended tragically, Palestinian Christians were caught in the middle: the Romans considered them Jews, the Jews considered them apostates. Many of them fled to other Christian communities around the Empire, taking with them their collections of Jesus' sayings and deeds. To an audience outside Palestine—used to the more philosophical message from the missionaries—the effect of these concrete stories and statements of Jesus must have been tremendous. And the addition of this historical-mythic material with their more theological material was responsible in no small part for the writing of the gospels of Luke and Matthew.

Probably during the Jewish War of 66–70 A.D., the version of the Good News according to Mark was already being written, very likely in Rome. Hearing word of the carnage of the war, seeing all around him Christians persecuted by orthodox Jews and by Nero, Mark could not have helped but think that the details of the End-Time prophecies of Jesus were on the verge of being literally fulfilled.

But other concerns were reflected in his gospel as well, and with a host of recollections from Peter (whose interpreter he very likely was), a brief account of the Passion, scattered anecdotes, sayings, and brief collections of writings, he set out to construct a book that would explain "The Way" of Christian belief. Nearly 20 percent of Mark's gospel (about 117 verses) is taken up with so-called controversy stories which give us a very good idea of the issues that troubled the people in the persecuted Christian community for whom Mark was writing.

Mark's passion account (which he inherited) attempted to answer the very obvious question: Why did Jesus die? And why did he die such an apparently shameful death? Why would the people desire his death and why would God allow it? To these questions Mark attempts an answer. First of all, Jesus died because the Jewish leaders refused to believe him and, out of envy (15:10), handed him over to Pilate. Jesus died because he willed to die: Jesus said, "For the Son of Man himself did not come to be served but to serve, and to give his life as a ransom for many" (10:45). If Jesus did not die and rise, we would never have known that we too would die but arise.

But most important, Jesus died because God willed it and had expressed the divine will throughout the Hebrew scriptures: Jesus said, "Yes, the Son of Man is going to his fate, as the scriptures say he will" (14:21a); and in the garden, "Abba (Father)!' he said, 'Everything is possible for you. Take this cup away from me. But let it be as you, not I, would have it." And at the crucifixion the details are taken from the Psalms of the Suffering Servant.

In the controversy stories which occupy almost a fifth of his gospel, Mark attempts to answer other questions using the literary device of placing the question in the mouths of Jesus' antagonists, the scribes and pharisees, and giving either the answer Jesus himself historically gave or one that was consistent with his message. These can be grouped under disputes which Mark's later audience had (1) with Jews, (2) the Greco-Roman environment, or (3) both. Remember, too, that these answers of Mark were not merely defensive against attack from Jews and Hellenists, but also offensive—seeking out converts and instructing the already converted. These are some of the questions Mark attempted to provide answers for in his gospel:

- *For Jews:* the Sabbath observance, divorce, the "greatest commandment," the Davidic descent of the Messiah, and food regulations.

- *For non-Jews:* the problem of paying tribute to Caesar when that money could be used immorally (like the moral problem of paying taxes for the Vietnam war or civil disobedience).

- *For both:* the source of Jesus' power and the source of his authority, the need for signs to prove beyond doubt Jesus was Lord, defense of eating with pagans and "sinners."

There were also other questions troubling his audience. For instance, who were the true leaders of the church? Mark's answer is simple: "the Twelve" (3:13–19). What was the relation of John the Baptizer's doctrine to Jesus' doctrine? It is clear to Mark that John was the "Elijah" who was to return to prepare the way of the Lord; he was not Jesus' rival but his herald. Was martyrdom for the sake of others (like Jesus' martyrdom) the only true test of discipleship? Throughout the gospel, Mark's

Jesus gives a far less terrifying demand—faith in Jesus as Lord: humbling oneself, giving a cup of water, living in peace, being wary of riches, childlike vulnerability. In other words, the true test of Christian discipleship is complete renunciation of self-ishness for Christ's sake and the sake of the Kingdom. Still, for Mark's audiences in and around the Rome of the ferocious Nero, complete renunciation might well mean martyrdom.

But one can imagine the effect of this gospel on meetings of the frightened, persecuted Christians in Rome and throughout the Empire, in danger at any moment of being hung up as living torches in Nero's gardens or thrown to the beasts in the arena. Here is a Jesus, compassionate and willing to help, a friend of sinners; here is a Jesus, hated and despised, betrayed by his friend, deserted by his disciples and sent to shameful death at the hands of Jews and Romans. Surely it was a precious document to them.

But besides the Apocalypse of Chapter 13, the Passion account, and the controversies handed on to him, Mark is quoted by some as having a fourth major source of material for his version of the message: the testimony of Peter himself. Papias of Hieropolis, writing in the early second century, stated:

> "When Mark became Peter's interpreter, he wrote down accurately although not in order, all that he remembered of what the Lord had said or done. For he had not heard or followed the Lord, but later, as I said, [heard and followed] Peter, who used to adapt his teaching to the needs [of the moment], without making any sort of arrangement of the Lord's oracles. Consequently, Mark made no mistake in thus writing down certain things as he remembered them. For he was careful not to omit or falsify anything of what he heard."
>
> *(JBC 42:2)*

And Mark's gospel was written (65–70) only a few years after Peter's death in Rome (around 64 A.D.). When it was written, the character of Peter had been transfigured by martyrdom, and it is easy to see how readily those threatened by persecution would understand this model (not ideal) disciple who believed so fiercely yet doubted so often, who loved Jesus dearly yet failed so frequently, who stood breathless at the Transfiguration and snored through the agony in the Garden, who three times denied the Jesus he loved and yet wept bitterly at his weakness and became a missioner of the message of the resurrection.

The Jesus of Mark is the Son of God, equipped with divine knowledge and power. But he is also the one-time Jewish teacher and prophet, with human feelings and limited knowledge and power. Divinity and humanity interpenetrate each other in Jesus in an inseparable unity. He is more than the Messiah; he is the Son of God. Mark does not reflect how one could be both God and human at the same time, nor how God's Son arrived or departed. But in his rugged Greek prose—so different from Luke's—he affirmed his belief in a forthright tone that seemed to say, "Don't ask me to explain it, but that's the way things are." It is the same tone as Peter's answer to Jesus' question of who they thought Jesus was. "Peter spoke up and said, 'You are the Christ.'" Period. It is the same tone as the tough Gentile centurion's at the cross in the statement that climaxes Mark's gospel: "Truly, this man was the Son of God." Period. Mark wrote, as we say today, "in your face."

Divisions of the New Testament

The following chart should not be taken as a hard-and-fast, conclusively historical list—like the dates and succession of

American presidents. The writers did not have our modern passion for dating and accuracy. If Paul himself, for instance, is not the author of the letters to Timothy and Titus, they should probably be dated in the 80's. However, most scholars would accept this tentative list, each with his or her own reservations here and there. (See *JBC*, 67:57.)

Approximate Dates of Composition
(as opposed to their printed order in our Bibles)

EARLY 50's	1 Thessalonians
	2 Thessalonians
LATE 50's	Galatians
	1 Corinthians
	2 Corinthians
	Romans
	Philippians (?)
EARLY 60's	Philippians (?)
	Philemon
	Colossians
	Ephesians
MID 60's	**MARK**
	1 Timothy
	Titus
	2 Timothy
	1 Peter
70's-80's	**MATTHEW**
	LUKE–ACTS
	Jude
	James
	Hebrews
90's	**JOHN**
	Apocalypse
	Epistles of John

Chapter Eight

COMPOSITION OF THE GOSPELS

As I sit here trying to map out this chapter on how the gospel texts emerged, I suddenly realize how like the evangelists' work is my own work in writing this book. I am not a scripture scholar in any sense of the word; I am a teacher, trying to take something I really believe in and want to share, something I've studied a good deal on a graduate level, and put it into terms that are understandable to readers who want to read the gospels on their own, without a teacher, but who have had no specific training—in terms that will not simplify-and-falsify.

So I sit here at a desk littered with all kinds of books and notes from other books. They vary in their heaviness, both academic and physical. There is the *Jerusalem Bible,* Perrin's *Introduction,* the *Jerome Biblical Commentary,* Grant's book on the origin and growth of the gospels, and Throckmorton's *Gospel Parallels.* I have books that are only about Luke, books that are only about the parables. I even have the Monarch Notes on the New Testament—just in case! But none of them is geared to my audience, to those who have left their religious education back in school. Even the texts that are geared for college students seem to require something more like a seminary background.

So I read them all. I borrow a bit here, a bit there, follow this writer's outline where it suits my purposes, someone else's when that fits. Mostly, I have to piece together what all these people say, add my own insights and my knowledge of the receptivities of my particular audience, then write away. For instance, the blending of literary and biblical uses of figurative language at the beginning of this book is something I have never seen anywhere else, but when I checked it with friends in biblical studies, they said it was not only justified but useful.

Much the same thing happens with all scholarship. There are a few geniuses, like Einstein or Teilhard, whose work is at the outer reaches of human knowledge. Their publications are so technical, so involved, so abstract that they can communicate only to a few others who, though they themselves do not do original work on that creative level, can still comprehend these new ideas and "translate them downward" to college students, government officials, readers of more academic magazines. Once again, these students "translate downward" for high school students and Sunday supplements and news magazines. In this way, the ideas gradually percolate down to the "ordinary" person in the street—in a highly diluted form, but hopefully in an honest form.

The same thing, or something like it, happens with the gospels. Jesus, the God–Man, revealed his earthshaking message of resurrection. Then Spirit-filled souls like Paul and Peter and the evangelists did their best to "translate downward" this message they understood so well to ordinary people. And what we as individuals receive in our turn is limited only by our intellectual abilities on the one hand and our depth of faith on the other. This is where the analogy to scientific writing breaks down, because the apostles and evangelists were not only trying to pass on ideas, but were also actively engaged in trying to stir up an inner, personal response to it.

Moreover, the evangelists were not helped (or burdened) by our present-day armory of scientific research: accurate statistics, government reports, official documents, catalogues, surveys, etc. They had the testimony of eyewitnesses and a few scrolls containing an outline of the Passion and the founding of the Eucharist, plus a few collections of miracle stories, controversy stories, parables, and perhaps a skeleton of a discourse on the coming of the End. And, of course, the Hebrew scripture.

This is what Mark had in front of him when he sat down to write the first gospel: some information, but more importantly a purpose. Mark and the other evangelists did not pretend to have the studied objectivity of a television newscaster when they sat down to report the Good News. They had a point to make, and each one made that point in his own particular way. Even today, though modern journalists strive for objectivity, some of their personal convictions and opinions certainly "leak" through, for instance when they are reporting a story on abortion, in the choice of a particular word rather than another or even in the choice of which stories deserve putting on the air. Listen carefully, and you can usually tell which side the reporter is on.

The evangelists, too, picked and chose from the materials they had inherited—as I pick and choose what materials would help my audience and what would merely confuse them uselessly. All of the evangelists wanted to get across the same basic point: the Good News about the Kingdom which had been sown and was growing. But each presented it in his own way, with an eye to his particular audience and inescapably influenced by his own personal insights into the message.

This will be clearer if we look at an actual passage from the Passion, where the three synoptic gospels are most alike.

MATTHEW 27	MARK 15	LUKE 23
[51]And behold, the curtain of the temple was torn in two, from the top to bottom; and the earth shook and the rocks were split.	[38]And the curtain of the temple was torn in two from top to bottom.	[see v. 45]

[52]The tombs also were opened, and many bodies of the saints who had fallen asleep were raised. [53]And coming out of the tombs after his resur-

rection they went into the holy city and appeared to many.

54When the centurion and those who were with him, keeping watch over Jesus, saw the earthquake and what took place, they were filled with awe, and said, "Truly this was the Son of God!"

39And when the centurion, who stood facing him, saw that he thus breathed his last, he said, "Truly this man was the Son of God!"

47Now when the centurion saw what had taken place, he praised God, and said, "Certainly this man was innocent!" 48And all the multitudes who assembled to see the sight, when they saw what had taken place, returned home, beating their breasts.

In this and subsequent exercises, always begin in the middle column with Mark, since Mark was written first and since both Matthew and Luke were merely writing updated versions of Mark's original. Then you can see how Matthew and Luke *edited* Mark for their own unique audiences.

Take a pencil and draw a solid line under words and phrases where the three or even two writers agree verbatim (although this is only second-best compared to doing it in the Greek original). Then draw a broken line under words and phrases that are more or less the same, just a difference in vocabulary or style. Finally, circle the places where only one of the three has an entry.

It is obvious that all three have *similarities.* They are all speaking of the same historical event: the death of Jesus. It is also obvious that the three have common details: the centurion and the people and their reactions to Jesus' death. But there are just as obvious *differences:*

• *Luke* has already put the detail of the torn curtain in his verse 45, before Jesus died. The event itself is probably only symbolic rather than the recording of an actual historical occurrence. This curtain hung in front of the Holy of Holies which symbolized the most sacred place in the Jewish cult. But why does Luke put it *before* Jesus' death rather than after as the other two did? Probably to say in symbolic terms that it was Judaism which was defeated at this moment and not Jesus.

• *Matthew* adds far more of these symbolic apocalyptic details: an earthquake, tombs opening and yielding up their dead, and Hebrew saints coming to life again after the resurrection of Jesus. Throughout his gospel, Matthew has a fondness for the apocalyptic form; he's really the "Stephen Spielberg" of the evangelists! The earthquake (which Old Testament poetry said figuratively were the footsteps of Yahweh passing by) is a sign that says God is leaving Israel behind. Also it is surely one of the signs of the beginning of the Day of Yahweh when the remnant of Israel would be freed. Moreover, through this symbol of the arisen dead, he can connect the resurrection of the believer with the resurrection of Jesus. That is why the Messiah had to die. Matthew was speaking to a Jewish audience who would grasp these allusions more readily than Gentiles or ourselves.

• Note carefully the declaration after Jesus' death. Mark, writing primarily for Gentiles, has this supreme declaration come from the lips of a Gentile Roman. Matthew, writing for Jews, says the testimony came not only from the Roman centurion but also from "those who were with him," other Roman soldiers who testified in words, which the Jews of Jesus' time would not. Moreover, the holy Jewish dead testified to Jesus' divinity by their "rising." Luke, writing for an educated Hellenistic audience, has the official Roman witness, the centurion, declare that he was certainly innocent—i.e., not guilty of any crime against the Roman state. And the "multitudes," the Jews, return to their homes acknowledging their guilt.

Each of the three tells of the same event, but each from a different point of view, for a different audience, and with a different purpose. Historically, who knows what the people who actually stood at the cross thought or said? The point is that Jesus actually did die, and that event and its aftermath, the resurrection, called for a response.

The gospels of Matthew, Mark, and Luke are called the "synoptic gospels," from the Greek word *synoptikos,* "seeing the whole thing together." It is the same root as for "synopsis." They tell much the same story in much the same way, and they can be set in parallel columns, as they were above, so that all three can be "seen together." The Gospel of John is the same basic story, too, but told from such a different point of view and with such a mystical, theological tone that we will not deal with it further in these pages except incidentally.

Similarities. The first three gospels have more or less the same content. They report many of the same words and deeds of Jesus, the same miracles, parables, discussions, and events. In some sections, all three will be verbally almost identical; in others, two will be identical. A glance at a book like Throckmorton's *Gospel Parallels*, which lines up the passage from the Passion above, makes this visually apparent.

The plot arrangement of the three gospels is also more or less parallel: The activities of the Baptist are described, Jesus is baptized by him and enters the desert where Satan (the symbol of worldly selfishness) tempts him to throw over his mission and join "everybody else." Jesus then begins his public life, preaching and healing in Galilee, and finally begins his last journey to Jerusalem and to his death and resurrection. The accounts of the Passion are where the three are most nearly identical.

The language is frequently exactly the same, even in places where all three agree on an Old Testament quotation *against* the Septuagint translation, the Greek version which Hellenistic Jews accepted. Sometimes all three will use the same unusual Greek syntax or the same comparatively rare Greek words.

Differences. Some speeches and events are recounted by only two; others are used by only one. Sometimes two accounts of the same event will be quite different, in emphasis and details chosen. Mark, for instance, has no account of Jesus' birth, while Matthew and Luke do. Even then, the two who do describe Jesus' birth and infancy differ widely. For example, Matthew has the Magi but no shepherds; Luke has shepherds but no Magi.

Even though the general progression of events is parallel in all three, there are some differences in arrangement of materials too. Where one author groups a clump of material together in one place, another may scatter it throughout his work. Matthew organizes his materials into five great discourses, each focusing on a common theme. Luke, however, organizes his materials around a single journey toward Jerusalem. Even individual sections are organized differently. One need only see the differences in the versions of the Our Father or the Beatitudes to recognize this.

Form Criticism:
The Gospel Writers as Collectors

How did all this happen? One way to approach the question is called *form criticism*. It is a highly technical, scholarly, scientific study of the linguistic forms of the Greek New Testament. It tries to discern beneath strange Greek sentence structures the original Aramaic in which Jesus or the very earliest community stated the original orally, before it was ever written down. It also studies additions to the original—like experts peeling away one layer of paint after another to get down to the original painting. This can be determined, for instance, by customs which came later than the time of Jesus or were proper to cultures outside Palestine. Further, they study concerns and questions brought to Jesus that did not actually arise until after his death. From their linguistic studies, form critics isolate various literary forms Jesus used in teaching: narratives, discourses, sayings, parables, miracle stories, interpretations of scripture, debates, etc. By studying the developments of such literary forms in other non-Jewish writings, they can show how not only the form was adapted in later years, but also the content.

Form criticism treats the evangelists as *collectors,* and their science tries to see how the synoptics' materials came to them. Within the texts they can pick out the remnants of material which was most likely organized and structured *before* it came into the evangelist's hands. They can see, for instance, chains of material linked together by a word-clue—much like the material of a modern stand-up comic which goes from a joke about one's mother-in-law in a car to a joke about a car in a crash, to an airplane crash, to a flight attendant joke, and on and on. The subject matter of the jokes has nothing in common, but one word from one joke hooks into one word in the next—because it's easier for the comic to remember them that way. The teachers and preachers in the early church probably used the same gimmick.

Scholars can also discern clumps of material grouped around a common subject, even though Jesus may have said the individual sentences at different times. They can isolate, too, passages which look as if they may have been drawn up for liturgical purposes in the early community or as handbooks for new converts. This does not mean that the gospels are just made up of bits and pieces, one-liners Jesus got off at various times and places. He was a teacher, and his audiences, as we said, had far better developed memories than we have.

Patterns begin to emerge. These scholars discover certain principles at work in the three versions of the one gospel. For instance, wherever the three agree, it is the order of Mark which rules. Matthew's and Mark's versions may agree against Luke's, but Matthew and Luke never agree against Mark. That sounds as complicated as a math formula, but it really is not. In the passage we saw above from the Passion, Mark and Matthew have the curtain torn after Jesus' death; Luke has it before. Mark and Luke omit the apocalyptic symbols of the earthquake and the opening tombs; Matthew includes them. Mark and Matthew have the centurion say "Son of God;" Luke has him say "innocent."

The point is that Luke and Matthew never agree *against* Mark. They may have material Mark does not have at all, where the texts in Luke and Matthew will be almost identical (the "Q" source). But there is no place where all three treat the same passage in which Mark has one version and Matthew and Luke agree on a different version. This consistent pattern of agreement not only in the overall sequence of events but in actual verbal agreement shows that the gospel of Mark was written first and that Matthew and Luke had a copy of Mark on their desks as they wrote.

In the diagram on the facing page, the three synoptic gospels are shown in boxes. But as the lines indicate, these final editions resulted from transmission first by oral communication, then through various written collections to the evangelist.

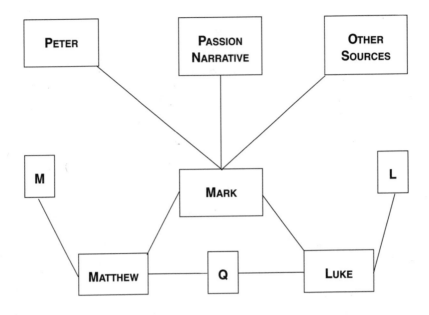

The circled letters are:

Q = The sayings source we have already seen, about 250 verses common to Luke and Matthew but not found in Mark.

M = Material found in Matthew alone, coming from a source or sources unknown to either Mark or Luke.

L = Material found in Luke alone, coming from a source or sources unknown to either Mark or Matthew.

Therefore,

Mark = Peter's recollections + a Passion outline + other sources + Old Testament.

Matthew = Mark + the Q collection + M, a source or sources unknown to Mark or Luke (e.g., Magi at the Nativity).

Luke = Mark + the Q collection + L, a source or sources unknown to Mark or Matthew (e.g., shepherds at the Nativity).

Therefore, some sections of the synoptic gospels are common to all three. These sections were originally in Mark and were included (edited) in Matthew's and Luke's new edition of Mark. In a large part, Matthew and Luke have edited, revised, abridged, and amplified Mark.

Furthermore, there are sections of Matthew and Luke which are so close verbally that they must be using another common source (Q), which was apparently not available to Mark (since he does not include such good material).

Still further, there are sections both in Matthew and in Luke that are unique to each of them, which shows that each of them had his own special collections of material (L for Luke's source and M for Matthew's) which was unavailable to the other.

Finally, we cannot omit the fact (as we will see with redaction criticism) that each of the three synoptics felt free to alter even the common material, interpret it differently, and fabricate further symbolic statements (e.g., Matthew's earthquake) which furthered his personal overall purpose in writing his version of the message.

As a result of their researches, then, form critics believe they can isolate more than a few stages ("layers") in the composition of "the gospel before the gospels," clumps of material that had been formulated in various communities during the thirty years between the resurrection and the time the gospels were beginning to be written.

But form criticism is not enough. The evangelists were not mere robots or computers assembling data. They were themselves Spirit-filled men, just as Paul and Peter had been. There is behind their separate works a recognizable person whose individual concerns and emphases are apparent throughout the individual book and unify it as the product of one man's single vision of the common data, no matter where these had been or in what form they had been before they came to him.

Redaction Criticism: The Gospel Writers as Editors

Redaction criticism treats the evangelists as *authors* and tries to see what the synoptics did to the material handed down to them. In studying dominant themes proper to each evangelist, differing plot structure, different use of the same characters, and especially what they add which the others don't have, critics see three very different human beings at work on the same basic message and even on the same basic sources. In knowing each of the three as a personality, the ordinary reader can get far more richness from reading a gospel by knowing how each version was written from a personal viewpoint.

Mark: The Roman Realist

It is too bad our translations of the gospels seem done by some kind of unbiased committee, rather than by individuals who could bring out the flavor of each evangelist's Greek. And they often resort to bland acceptability; for instance, in Mark's gospel, the Greek verb Jesus uses to calm the storm at sea is not some genteel word like, "Be calm" or "Be still." It's far closer to our "Shut up!" Mark is the briefest of the gospels, with a severe outline and a rugged style, spare and without embellishments. Mark has a job to do, and he does not have the same amount of time for Matthew's extensive theologizing or Luke's elegant style. As you read, notice how almost childish his style is, "And then . . . and then . . . ," as if he's rattling on breathlessly with the Roman soldiers rattling his door latch.

Mark is stern, facing the desperate issues confronting the faithful in a persecuted church, a people perhaps even facing martyrdom. He must persuade his audience to hang on, despite the inducements of the pagans to give in and live a materialist life—or face the lions.

He is less sympathetic to Judaism than Matthew or Luke; in fact he does not betray much knowledge of Judaism. That is not the principal problem facing him and his audience. Instead, he builds his gospel as the revelation of the messianic secret: Jesus slowly, slowly unveiling his real self to the disciples. It is amazing to see how frequently he describes Jesus' cures as cures of blindness, external physical blindness as a symbol of internal self-blindedness. And the messianic secret is gradually revealed in three climactic moments: (1) Peter's recognition of Jesus as the Messiah (8:29), (2) Jesus' reply at his trial that he is indeed "the Son of the Blessed One," (14:62), and finally (3) the climactic, forthright opening of the centurion's eyes: "Truly, this was the Son of God!" (15:39).

Matthew:
The Jewish Theologian-Teacher

Matthew—and Matthew alone—writes the parable of the householder: "Every scribe who has been trained for the Kingdom of God is like a householder who brings out of his treasure what is new and what is old" (13:52). He could be describing himself, offering his readers the treasures of both Old and New Covenants. Indeed, he could have been a former scribe or a rabbi himself, steeped in the Hebrew scriptures. His gospel is filled with Old Testament quotations and allusions, in an attempt to prove—doubtless to a Jewish audience—that the promise of the law and the prophets has been fulfilled, that Jesus is the Messiah, and that the Christian community is the seed of the New Israel.

After the disastrous fall of Jerusalem in 70 A.D., the orthodox Jew saw the land of his fathers lying in heaps. His Temple and its Sadducee priesthood had disappeared. For him, it was almost literally the end of the world as he knew it. The only thing left was to strengthen what remained, thus many of the scribes and pharisees retired to the town of Jamnia and began to study and reorganize the law and its interpretations. Henceforth, Judaism could not be focused on a Temple that no longer existed, but it would carry on as a religion centered in the school and the synagogue. Thus it has remained since that time until our own day.

Matthew attempted the same kind of study of the gospel message as the scribes were doing of the Law. Reflecting on the message of the Kingdom and on the data handed down to him from the earliest days, he wrote what was equivalently a Christian supplement to the Hebrew scriptures. In five discourses, like the five books of the Hebrew Pentateuch, he set out to develop his astonishing insight that Jesus is the new Moses, but an even greater teacher. Jesus is the Messiah of Old Testament hopes—not a warrior or prophet or priest in the literal way that they expected, but all those things summed up and transfigured by his role as the long-prophesied suffering servant of Yahweh.

Despite his rabbinic methods, Matthew is the most violently anti-pharisaic of all the evangelists—just as the converted pharisee,

Paul, was. Reading the woes that Jesus calls down on the
pharisees in Matthew's twenty-third chapter is enough to make
one shudder. The other synoptics show Jesus railing at pharisaic
hypocrisy, but none does it as emphatically as Matthew. And
these woes will fall on them because they rejected the Messiah.

Matthew's interests are Jewish: the Law, the messianic hope,
the fulfillment of prophecy, the duties of worship, prayer,
fasting, and almsgiving. Although he agrees with Paul about the
worldwide dimension of the message outside Judaism, he has
no sympathy with the seemingly wide-open interpretation Paul
had of the freedom of the sons of God. With typical teacher's
organization, he gathers his material before the Passion into five
great discourses of Jesus: (1) on discipleship (The Sermon on
the Mount); (2) on apostleship and spreading the word, once it's
learned; (3) on the hidden revelation (The Parables of the
Kingdom); (4) on church administration; (5) on the fulfillment
of the Kingdom in the day of Yahweh—and then the Passion,
the beginning of the Kingdom.

Luke: The Hellenistic Storyteller

Luke-Acts—which were undoubtedly written by the same
writer (both begin addressing "Theophilus")—takes up about
one-quarter of the whole New Testament. It is a sweeping
study of the historic message, first of Jesus, ending in Jerusalem,
then of Peter and Paul and the early community, ending in
Rome, the center of the known world. And it is told by a poet-
historian of elegant style and wonderfully sensitive humanity.

Only in Luke do we get the table talk, the friendliness, the
great parables of human kindness and goodness (like The Good
Samaritan and The Prodigal Son). Only in Luke are the
harshness and loathsomeness of Jesus' treatment during the
Passion toned down; one might almost suspect that Luke

cannot tolerate thinking such a Person could be so treated. The author of Luke's version has an observant eye for mannerisms, reactions, hidden motivations. And he has a broadminded openness to all groups and peoples: swineherds, Samaritans, lepers, publicans, soldiers, shepherds, prostitutes, the poor. It is interesting to check a list like Throckmorton's, which parallels the three gospels, and see the stories and parables that Luke has which the other two synoptics do not: the shepherds at Bethlehem, the widow at Nain, the Good Samaritan, Martha and Mary, the blessedness of Jesus' mother, the Prodigal Son, the Rich Man and Lazarus, healing the ten lepers, little Zaccheus in his sycamore tree, the disciples' pitiful armory of only two swords, the disciples on the road to Emmaus, and the Ascension of Jesus. Luke's gospel is kind.

Luke has a sympathy for Judaism, but his introduction to Theophilus which opens his gospel hints that he aims to attract and interest cultured readers—both to find converts and to ward off suppression by the Romans. He takes great pains to show his specific audience that there was nothing politically subversive or politically revolutionary about Jesus or his followers: after all, they had only two swords! Only Luke has the Roman procurator, Pilate, declare officially and explicitly, "I find no crime in this man." In Mark, Pilate orders Jesus' death "to satisfy the [Jewish] crowd"; in Matthew it is "out of fear of a riot"; but in Luke it is "to answer the demand of the Jews."

These are three different men, bringing their own special talents, interests, and insights to the materials handed down to them—some of which they all had available to them (at least through Mark), some of which Matthew and Luke shared, some of which Matthew and Luke had independently of one another. But their special interests did not blind them to the needs beyond their particular audiences. After all, it was only Matthew, the Jew, who included the Gentile Magi, and it was

only Luke, the Hellenist, who included the Jewish shepherds—
as the official witnesses to the birth of Jesus. And the aim of all
three was fundamentally the same: to present the same multi-
faceted Lord and his message of liberation from death.

Part Four

THE SYNOPTIC PASSIONS

Chapter Nine

THE ARREST OF JESUS

Why Begin at the End?

The Gospel of Luke is 24 chapters long: the first 21 chapters cover thirty years of Jesus' life; the last three chapters cover two and a half days. For this reason, someone has rightly said that each gospel is "a Passion narrative preceded by a biography." That's right. And there's a reason.

As we have said, the Passion is the most primitive gospel narrative. Sayings of Jesus circulated (the Beatitudes, the Our Father, the words of consecration at the Last Supper) and were memorized and even gathered into written collections. But the people in the early church were above all "witnesses to the resurrection" (Acts 1:22, 2:32, 3:15, etc., 1 Corinthians 15:14, Romans 10:9). That is the Good News; that's what they celebrated at their weekly eucharists. For a while, then, that Good News was enough.

But one does have to ask questions. If Jesus rose from the dead, it follows as the night the day that he had to die first, right? How did he die? Why did he die? "I thought you said he was God!" And so, very brief oral collections were drawn up gathering together the details of the most crucial and focal moments leading up to the event: the resurrection.

The Passion was the first formal narrative composed about the life of Jesus—the first attempt at more than random recollections of things Jesus did. It had a beginning which showed the characters and the tensions between them; a *catalytic moment,* some event that thrust into the tensions and triggered the action of the story (Judas's betrayal); a gradually building series of scenes showing the interplay between the protagonist and his antagonists (arrest, Sanhedrin trial, Roman trial); a climax where the hero could still escape (Pilate's reluctance to kill Jesus); a last confrontation in which the "bad guys" seemed to win (Jesus' death); and a happy ending where the protagonist abruptly foils his antagonists (the empty tomb).

How does the shrewd detective know that the Passion was the first narrative developed about the life of Jesus—and not some other section of his life, like the infancy narratives or the journey toward Jerusalem? We have no certainty; nobody sat down and wrote out how the gospels were gradually gathered together. But there are some heavy clues.

First, we know how important stories tend to be filled out. When the Watergate news first broke, it was just a brief news story about some men caught in the Democratic National Headquarters. But over the course of two years, look at the volumes upon volumes of data that grew out of it! It was like pulling on a single thread and dragging out acres of unsuspected yarns.

But the more reporters unearth solid data and the more writers organize and interpret them, the more versions you get. Some reporters pull this particular bit of data first; some hold it for a snappy climax to an article. You find this same practice throughout the gospels. There are certain basic chronological facts that are unchangeable: Jesus began with his baptism by John in the Jordan, went around preaching, and ended on a cross in Jerusalem. Those are the skeletal facts, and all good reporters and evangelists have to adhere to them.

But since there were no diaries or logs of Jesus' activities as there were in Watergate, it didn't make that much difference when Jesus said such and such or did such and such; the fact he did it and the probing for what it meant were far more important. Therefore, you'll find Luke has Jesus picking all twelve apostles and then giving the Beatitudes sermon at the base of a hill; Matthew, on the other hand, has Jesus picking four fishermen, giving substantially the same but an expanded Beatitudes sermon on top of a hill, and then choosing the other apostles later.

What difference when or where, as long as he chose them? And the Beatitudes are as true whether they were first spoken on the top of a hill or at the bottom of another hill entirely. Both Matthew and Luke had their own sources of information on exact times and places—sometimes conflicting. But more important, since the events themselves were more significant than the time and place, the first writers were primarily interested in discovering what meaning the deeds and sayings of Jesus could have for the Christian and the interested pagan. Therefore, both Matthew and Luke arranged those events into a sequence which more fully enriched the total appreciation of that same Christian message each shared with the other, in his own way.

Strangely, though, unlike the organization of the episodes in Jesus' public life, the Passion sections of all four gospels are not very different at all from one another. If you look at the gospels of Mark and John before the Passion, the outlines are very different. But when you come to the entry into Jerusalem, all four gospels begin to become far more similar in their order of progression. These events—or this one event as a developing wholeness—was far too sacred to juggle around with too much. As a result, Mark still differs from John, and somewhat even from Matthew and Luke, up until the arrest in the Garden. From then on—with little personal adjustments here and there—they are singing precisely the same song in the same rhythm, moving through the same places at the same times with the same sayings.

Even John's style, which is the most distinctive throughout, changes at the moment of the arrest. All four writers are handling material that has already become sacred and established in the memories of their listeners. The basic account—beginning with the arrest—had been formulated very early in the primitive church: solemn, schematic, and written in rather good Greek. Each of the four writers fiddled a bit here and there, but they wouldn't tamper with substantials.

Since the gospels' structures are most similar in the Passion accounts (from the arrest onward), the slight differences may more easily betray the particular interests and intentions of each author. So we begin with the Passion accounts.

A further reason why the Passion accounts would very likely be the first narratives written by the early church is that they deal with a problem the early church must have faced—a problem also far more important than absolute stop-watch accuracy. In dealing with converts and with Christians of flagging faith, the early church had to cope with the scandal of the cross, the apparent failure of Christ (and therefore of God) on Calvary.

Even during his lifetime, Jesus faced angered disbelief—even from Peter, his most typical disciple—when he predicted the degradation he saw was inevitable for him. But Peter's reaction both to the predictions and to the actuality of the Passion was the normal human reaction: "No! He's too good, too special! It's hard enough to accept a God who can let a good person suffer sickness and death, but not him! And surely not walking into it with his eyes wide open. He's the best of us! No God could be good and allow that, much less seem to demand it."

In the light of this inevitable reaction, it's surprising at first that the evangelists didn't play down the darkness and the horror of the Passion. (Luke softens it a touch here and there, but he will not avoid the unavoidable truth: It was ugly.) And yet the forthright way in which the writers handle the bruising contradictions of the God-man's last hours shows that from the beginning Christianity was not a religion either of unrelieved light or of evasion. The Passion, they realized, was not a brief and unfortunate little interlude that could be smiled over in a few well-chosen phrases. Nor on the other hand was it a defeat. It was an ugly combat—but an ultimately victorious combat. The cross is the crux of Christianity.

For this reason, the evangelists stress two things: first, Jesus' foreknowledge of the unavoidable climax and his free consent to it; and second, the constant recurrence of quotations from the Old Testament which show that, from the beginning, this particular fate was God's will for Christ himself. And remember that to the ears of a Jewish audience which from childhood had been steeped in the Old Testament, even a single word, even a similar rhythm of phrase brought echoes of the prophecies of the Passion. For the Gentiles of Luke's audience—including ourselves—who are not that familiar with the Old Testament, he and the other evangelists make explicit Old Testament references again and again. Granted these are only hints of the entire Hebrew passage referred to, but if you take the time to trace them from the footnotes in your text to the full Old Testament source, you will get an idea how this interweaving of the two testaments enrich one another and give the reader—then and now—a firm conviction of the purposeful evolution of humankind's destiny in the patient hands of God.

The Gospel Account

What you are about to read is not a biographical account of the last hours of a dead hero. You are about to study the testament of three men's faith in the risen Lord and in the Father who used him to destroy death.

One preliminary note: Although the evangelists are more fully parallel in the Passion accounts than they are anywhere else, this does not claim they are four verbally identical accounts. Despite their strong congruence, each one retains his particular perspective on the same story, his particular style, his particular "axe."

Mark gives the *kerygma*—the irreducible message of the early church. It is obvious from his helter-skelter style that he's rattling off the story orally, improvising, and that he is so filled with the excitement and the challenge of the thing that he doesn't care that his grammar's not too great, that he doubles back, that he scatter-shoots. He writes like an enthused high school freshman! Not only is he not afraid to stun his audience; he wants to. The cross is a scandal, but God wanted it that way!

Matthew speaks as the voice of the Christian people vs. the voice of the Israelite people. He is careful, clarifying Mark, orderly. He wants his audience to understand this happening and its place in God's slow working of humankind toward fulfillment.

Luke is more cautious even than Matthew. He wants to write with greater attention to style, to narrative "build," to meaningful juxtaposition. He is a Gentile with a sense of the structures and unities of Greek drama. But more than anything he wants to show how the first Christian reacted to defeat with the confidence of a victor—knowing, as Luke did, that many men and women among his audience would face just such accusers, just such judges, just such deaths, and just such resurrections. He is letting the reader "in" to the gospel, as the audience is let "in" to a play, to walk with Jesus. In a sense, he is writing a manual for martyrs.

Thus, there are three things to look for: the absolutely common elements to all three versions, the slightly different outlines, the clearly different emphases. Then we can ask, with such similarities, why does each stress what he does?

When reading the gospels in parallel, it is best to begin with Mark whose text the other two had before them as they wrote. Read the whole Mark text for each section and find where the logical divisions and transitions of each section occur; it's like dividing the scenes of a play into "beats" or "sub-scenes," signaled by the entrance of a new character or change of subject. In the pages which follow, these divisions will be made for you, but after a little practice it should not be difficult to do it for yourself. Draw a line across the three columns at each of these structural breaks, and concentrate your attention only on that small, manageable section before going on to the next.

In each of these smaller segments—no more than four or five verses—(1) underline first the exact correspondences with a solid line, then (2) the approximate correspondences with a broken line, and finally (3) circle the material unique to each. Read Mark first, then compare Matthew to Mark, then compare Luke to both. Knowing what each evangelist's interests and audience were, try to see why Mark pictured this situation as he did and then why Matthew and Luke varied Mark's text. If tag-phrases help to keep the three separate, think of Mark, the persecuted Roman realist; Matthew, the Jewish theologian-teacher; Luke, the Hellenistic storyteller who was defending the Christian community from suppression as "perpetrators of shameful deeds."

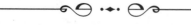

Jesus Taken Captive

MATTHEW 26	**MARK 14**	**LUKE 22**
[47]While he was still speaking, Judas came, one of twelve, and with him a great crowd with swords and clubs, from the chief priests and the elders of the people.	[43]And immediately, while he was still speaking, Judas came, one of the twelve, and with him a crowd with swords and clubs, from the chief priests and the	[47]While he was still speaking, there came a crowd, and the man called Judas, one of the twelve, was leading them.

scribes and the
elders.

⁴⁸Now the betrayer
had given them a
sign, saying, "The one
I shall kiss is the man;
seize him."

⁴⁴ Now the betrayer
had given them a
sign, saying, "The one
I shall kiss is the man;
seize him and lead
him away safely."

⁴⁹And he came up to
Jesus at once and
said, "Hail Master!"
And he kissed him.
⁵⁰Jesus said to him,
"Friend, why are you
here?" Then they
came up and laid
hands on Jesus and
seized him.

⁴⁵And when he came,
he went up to him at
once, and said,
"Master!" And he
kissed him.

⁴⁶And they laid hands
on him and seized
him.

He drew near to
Jesus to kiss him;
⁴⁸but Jesus said to
him, "Judas, would
you betray the Son of
man with a kiss?"

Unraveling the Meaning

First Beat: The Arrival

- Notice all the "ands" in Mark, rather than the more
  elegant connectives of the others. Why did both
  Matthew and Luke drop out "And immediately"?

- Judging from what little we've seen of Matthew so far, what reason could he have for adding "great," for omitting the scribes from the marauders, for sharpening the focus onto the elders "of the people"?

- What does "the man called" add to your feeling about Judas? And how is that feeling amplified by the fact Luke says Judas "was leading them"?

Second Beat: The Agreed Signal

- Jesus must have been known around the city. Why the need for a signal at all? Why does Luke omit it?

- Matthew repeats Mark verbatim but omits the last phrase. Why?

Third Beat: The Kiss and Seizure

- Why does Matthew omit "he went up"?

- What painful nuance is added by "Hail"? In Matthew's Last Supper (20:23–25), Jesus knows Judas is plotting. What further painful nuance is added by Jesus calling him "friend" and asking his reason?

- What reason could Luke, the gentlest of the synoptics, have for changing the actual kiss in Mark to only an attempt to kiss Jesus? Despite his omissions from Mark, why is his version even stronger?

MARK: First of all, when you are reading Mark this closely, you may be able to pick up the slightly out-of-kilter style, even in the English translation. Unlike the other two, his style is urgent, breathless, almost as if he were dictating it in a rage at what Judas was doing. "And immediately—while he was still speaking!" Notice, too, the awkward, "And when he came, he went up." In

MATTHEW, MARK, LUKE & YOU

the Greek it is literally translated: "And coming, immediately coming up to him." Compare it to the same phrases in Matthew who smoothes out the rugged, breathy style.

Finally, note that even though the action of "laying hands on Jesus" and "seizing" him are exactly the same, even Matthew keeps them separate as Mark had them. Why? Perhaps because the thought of such people touching Jesus was equally as repulsive as the thought of his being arrested.

MATTHEW: Notice how similar Matthew is to Mark. His only changes are to specify that it was a "great" crowd (Matthew has Spielberg tendencies) and to use the name "Jesus" to clear up the ambiguity of "him" and "he." Also he cleans up the messy style.

But Matthew does have a few significant additions and deletions. Perhaps Matthew omits scribes from the mob because he was a former scribe himself. He also omits Mark's puzzling "lead him away safely." Jesus wasn't going to be safe at all.

And he adds a remark of Jesus, "Friend, why are you here?" The reason is obvious: It heightens the enormity of what Judas is doing, leading enemies not to his own enemy or to a villain but to a man still large-hearted enough to call him "friend."

Although most versions translate this as "why are you here" or "why have you come," in Greek there is no verb in the sentence. Therefore, most commentators would prefer to remain with the less grammatical but more powerful half-sentence: "For what you have come!" or as we might say, "Friend, get on with it!"

LUKE says Judas was leading the crowd, not as its appointed head but as a bloodhound seeking out the prey, and he saves the identification of the members of the crowd until later, v. 52. A good plot device to keep the listener in suspense.

But the most significant omissions are the use of the kiss as a prearranged signal and the actual kiss itself. Perhaps Luke felt that, Jesus being as well-known as he was, the kiss was not necessary. Some have said that, since the Garden was dark and since the officials didn't want to arrest the whole group of disciples, Judas had used it as a signal. But Luke uses the kiss as the ordinary action by which two Jewish friends of the time would greet one another. The most focal omission is that he drops the words, "And he kissed him." Jesus prevented it, and perhaps Luke's customary "protectiveness" for Jesus refused to picture such a concretely revolting incident.

Like Matthew, Luke adds a reply of Jesus to Judas's attempt. But the significant difference is that in Luke's version Jesus knows only too clearly why Judas is there. What's more, he puts that action into a context far greater than an incident in a garden or even the betrayal of a friend. This is an action, for Luke, on a cosmic level. This is not just the arrest of a holy rabbi or even of a prophet. This is the betrayal of the Son of Man, whom the prophet Daniel saw coming on the clouds of heaven to take possession of his inheritance, the Kingdom.

The Attack on the Slave

Remember: (1) underline first the exact correspondences with a solid line, then (2) the approximate correspondences with a broken line, and finally (3) circle the material unique to each.

MATTHEW 26	MARK 14	LUKE 22
[51]And behold, one of those who were with Jesus stretched out his hand and drew his sword, and struck the slave of the high priest, and cut off his	[47]But one of those who stood by drew his sword, and struck the slave of the high priest and cut off his ear.	[49]And when those who were about him saw what would follow, they said, "Lord, shall we strike with the sword?" [50]And one of them struck the slave

ear. [52]Then Jesus said to him, "Put your sword back into its place; for all who take the sword will perish by the sword. [53]Do you think that I cannot appeal to my Father, and he will at once send me twelve legions of angels? [54]But how then should the scriptures be fulfilled, that it must be so?"

of the high priest and cut off his right ear. [51]But Jesus said, "No more of this!" And he touched his ear and healed him.

Unraveling the Meaning

- None of the three synoptics identifies the assailant, even Mark—one of whose sources was Peter himself. Where would you suspect we got the idea it was Peter?

- Mark says "one of those who stood by." Why is Matthew's version better at that point? Why does Luke have Jesus' followers ask the question whether they should offer physical resistance?

- Both Matthew and Luke have copies of Mark they are editing. Matthew brings in twelve legions of angels. How is that typical of him? Why would he resort to the Hebrew scriptures more than the other two?

- Why—again, typically—is Luke the only one who shows Jesus actually healing the slave's ear?

MARK is typically terse. Somebody pulled a sword and cut off the ear of the high priest's slave. That's that. No apologies, no criticism, either from Jesus or from Mark.

MATTHEW, improving on Mark, specifies that the assailant was actually one of Jesus' followers. Then he alone uses the incident for a statement from Jesus against violence as a solution to problems. But notice that Jesus does not object to violence as being immoral but as being utterly futile. In the light of the persecuted audience to whom he was writing, what do you suspect Matthew was "saying"? Matthew's point is that armed resistance—whether in Jesus' time or in Matthew's time—will prevent God's will (as expressed in the scriptures) from being fulfilled. Finally, it is obvious Jesus could have escaped this crowd, as he had done before, or even called heavenly power (the symbol of angels) to save him. But he would not. He chooses here to accept the will of the Father, as ordained in the scriptures and as executed here by the agents of the skeptical hierarchy.

LUKE shows the disciples asking Jesus if they should fight. In a verse previous to this episode, at the Last Supper (22:38), they have told Jesus about their entire armory: two swords. But someone of their number—only John says that it was Peter and that the slave's name was Malchus—draws a sword and attacks the slave. Only Luke says it was his right ear, and Matthew and Mark use the Greek word for "earlobe." It was not a huge battle!

Then Luke pictures Jesus saying, "No more of this!" Equivalently, Jesus is saying, "Hands off! You don't know what you're doing." This is roughly similar to Matthew's statement about using the sword, at that moment or in the future.

Then, only in Luke, in direct contrast to the use of violence, Jesus takes compassion on the hurt man and heals him. This is typically the Luke who himself had such compassion for the outcast. Earlier in their gospels, Matthew and Mark show Jesus performing miracles to show his power and the power of his Kingdom over "Satan" and his Kingdom. Typically, Luke shows Jesus performing this miracle solely out of human kindness for the wounded man. It is Luke, after all, who is the only evangelist who tells the story of the Good Samaritan.

Jesus' Submission

MATTHEW 26	**MARK 14**	**LUKE 22**
⁵⁵At that hour Jesus said to the crowds,	⁴⁸And Jesus said to them,	⁵²Then Jesus said to the chief priests and captains of the temple and elders, who had come out against him,
"Have you come out as against a robber, with swords and clubs to capture me?	"Have you come out as against a robber, with swords and clubs to capture me?	"Have you come out as against a robber, with swords and clubs?
Day after day I sat in the temple teaching, and you did not seize me.	⁴⁹Day after day I was with you in the temple teaching and you did not seize me.	⁵³When I was with you day after day in the temple, you did not lay hands on me. But this is your hour, and the power of darkness."
⁵⁶But all this has taken place that the scriptures of the prophets might be fulfilled." Then all the disciples forsook him and fled.	"But let the scriptures be fulfilled." And they all forsook him and fled.	
	⁵¹And a young man followed him, with	

nothing but a linen
cloth about his body;
and they seized him,
[52]but he left the linen
cloth and ran away
naked.

Unraveling the Meaning

- The major difference among the three versions is
  Mark's puzzling addition of the young man who ran
  away naked. Since Matthew and Luke have Mark's
  version, why would they omit mention of him? Look
  at the verse before. Why is it impossible that Mark can
  mean this young man to be a literal person?

- In the first beat, when Jesus asks why the officials have
  come out with armed soldiers, the three writers agree
  verbatim. What does this suggest about the words'
  authenticity?

- Considering Luke's Gentile audience, why would he
  be less interested in stressing that this was "to let the
  scripture be fulfilled"?

- Luke, who has omitted Judas kissing Jesus, also says
  nothing explicit about the disciples' desertion or of
  the mob laying hands on Jesus. Why?

MARK: The only addition Mark has is the puzzling little
picture he tacks onto the end of the episode: a young man
fleeing naked. Since Mark is so all-fired in a hurry and here
adds something no other gospel has, one must suspect a
purpose.

Perhaps one possibility emerges if you will allow a little Greek. The English verb "followed" does not really bring out the full meaning of the Greek verb Mark uses: *sunekoluthei*, which is really stronger, something like "shadowed" or "followed intimately." Who then is this young man who is "shadowing" Jesus?

The Greek word *sindon,* a fine unused linen cloth, and the Greek adjective *peribeblemenos,* "thrown about him," and the noun *neaniskos,* "young man," occur again later in Mark's gospel: When Mark treats the events of Easter morning, the women are greeted not by an angel (as in Matthew) or by two men (as in Luke) but by a "young man," *neaniskon,* with a white cloth "wrapped around him," *peribeblemenon.* The word for white cloth is not *sindon,* but it is a white cloth nonetheless.

The verbal similarities between this episode of the Marcan "streaker" and the episode after Jesus' death seem too close for coincidence. They must have some historical basis *or* else some symbolic significance. But why would Mark, so thrifty with words, include the escape of just one more of the disciples *after* "they *all* forsook him and fled"? Perhaps this "young man" is a mythic way of saying some greater truth, another way of describing the ultimate desertion: the loss of the sense of the Father's protecting power. Angels and young men are frequently used throughout the Old Testament as symbols of God's presence. If this young man in white who flees Jesus is a symbol of God's protective presence fleeing Jesus, then he is alone indeed. First his disciples desert him. Then the power of God's felt presence deserts him, too—to return only at the resurrection.

MATTHEW and **MARK** both stress that Jesus freely surrendered himself. The officials need not have sought him out in such a lonely place. The Passion narratives stress that the Jewish leaders did not want a public arrest, since they couldn't gauge the reaction of the populace—who had greeted Jesus with palms only a week before!

The disciples had offered to use force, but when Jesus rejected that, they didn't know what to do. So they ran.

LUKE has Jesus say, "This is your hour, and (this is) the power of darkness." The first half of the statement is merely a concession of this round to the Temple, but the second part shows that the Jewish officials themselves are pawns in the hands of a far greater force, the Kingdom of Satan, the power of darkness.

Remember that throughout the New Testament the battle is on a cosmic scale. "Satan" is the symbol of all that is selfish and self-destructive in human beings. And surely the Passion is a monument to man's self-destructiveness—the slaughter of the herald of the Good News of immortality.

In the earlier episode where Jesus is tempted by "Satan" in the desert, only in Luke (4:5) does the Tempter offer him *exousia,* "power, authority," if Jesus will fall down and adore him (i.e., selfishness). That is the same word Luke uses here: "the *exousia* of darkness." And at the end of the temptation scene in the desert, Luke alone says that Satan left him "to return at the appointed time." Here, in the garden, "This is the power of darkness" returning. This is the appointed time.

From the moment of the desert temptation to this moment of arrest, Jesus had gone about his business free of any kind of attack, as if there were a shield around him. Demons infesting possessed people cried out in torment at his approach. But during the Last Supper, the shields begin breaking down. Only Luke (22:3) says, "Then Satan entered into Judas, called Iscariot." Only Luke (22:31–32) connects Peter's denials with the Enemy's increasing power, readying for the kill: "Simon, Simon, behold. Satan demanded to have you, that he might sift you like wheat, but I have prayed for you in that your faith may not fail; and when you have turned again, strengthen your brethren."

There is a far stronger climax to Luke's version of this scene than the English translation delivers: "This is the power of darkness." This is in fact the critical moment, the crisis point. After the agony in the garden, Luke's hero has made up his mind; he is ready. The shields are down, and Jesus stands utterly alone and naked to his enemy.

This is not merely a struggle between an untamable rabbi and a handful of envious priests. This is a cosmic battle between the darkness and the light.

Summary of Different Emphases

MARK

Mark writes with simplicity and a kind of pell-mell breathless-ness. He gives very little information; just the bare story, as if he's saying, "Let's get to the climax!" In his account, Jesus says nothing to Judas and nothing to whoever cut off the slave's earlobe. But in his only solo addition Mark puts this episode into a cosmic scale just as solidly as the other two. He clearly associates this moment with the entire Old Testament myth of the way God deals with humankind. At this moment, the Son of Man stands deserted by his followers and by his own convic-tion of God's protective presence. It is just Jesus and the Enemy.

MATTHEW

Stylistically, Matthew smoothes out Mark's rough Greek prose. But his version of the scene shows Jesus as being more than the silent sufferer of Mark's version. He speaks both to Judas and to the swordsman-disciple (whom only John names as Peter), and uses the incident to make a point about the uselessness of violence, both in the time of Jesus and in the time of Matthew.

He explicitly shows that violence will frustrate the plan which God has been revealing to Israel for ages. Because it is the will of the Father that the Hero-Messiah suffer, Jesus freely chooses to accept that will and that suffering.

LUKE

Luke's is a more sophisticated narrative style. He shows first the crowd and only then its leader, whom one would pick out only after the initial shock of the group's intrusion. He saves disclosure of the identities of the mob until he has built up the scene, and he alone of the three says they *are* the temple priests rather than agents sent from the temple priests. Jesus is taken into custody only after the scene, not during it.

Luke is more delicate in his sensibilities and more protective of the person of Jesus, even in his reporting. There is no explicit reference in Luke to the fact that the disciples deserted Jesus, no actual kiss from Judas, but there is instead Jesus' kindly act of healing the wounded man.

Still there is the stern rebuke against using force, and as each of the evangelists does in his own way, Luke also places this event on a cosmic level by his declaration that this is the critical moment, when the power of darkness has unlimited access to Jesus.

Summary of Similarities

(1) All three have almost exactly the same skeletal outline or structure:

   a. The crowd and Judas

   b. The kiss

   c. Cutting off the ear

   d. Jesus addressing the crowd regarding their justification for the arrest

e. The cosmic dimension of the event

f. Jesus is taken away

(2) In all, the vagueness of the word "crowd" seems to indicate that no one was precisely sure who the particular individuals were or how large the group was.

(3) The kiss of Judas recalls to the well-trained Jewish ear the words of Psalm 55 (12–14, 20–21):

> Were it an enemy who insulted me,
>   I could put up with that;
> had a rival got the better of me,
>   I could hide from him.
> But you, a man of my own rank,
>   a colleague and a friend,
> to whom sweet conversation bound me
>   in the house of God! . . .
> He has attacked his friends,
>   he has gone back on his word;
> though his mouth is smoother than butter,
>   he has war in his heart;
> his words may soothe more than oil,
>   but they are naked swords.

Or, even more likely, Proverbs 27: "From one who loves, wounds are well-intentioned; from one who hates, kisses are ominous."

(4) When Jesus refuses them the only solution they know—fighting back—the disciples don't know what to do. This passive resistance makes no sense. So they desert him, although Luke discreetly leaves the reader to infer that from what follows. In all

three versions, it is fortunate Jesus didn't count on his followers for force, since the best they can do is an earlobe!

(5) All three have identical words in "Have you come out against a robber, with swords and clubs?"

(6) All three show Jesus asking why the officials did not capture him in some public place and, without waiting for a response, giving the answer himself. Although each does it in his own way, the answer given is one which raises this event far above the simple arrest of an innocent victim. This is a moment in a cosmic battle: In Mark and Matthew, this is the moment when all the Hebrew scriptures begin to focus; in Mark, it is the moment when Jesus' certitude about God's protecting presence deserts him; in Luke it is the moment when the battle between Jesus and the Enemy is joined. And in all three, Christ freely gives himself up to these self-important little men who, unknowingly, are merely the pawns of Jesus' real enemy.

Chapter Ten

THE SANHEDRIN TRIAL

Before going on to the separate sections of the Sanhedrin (high priest and elders) trial in the three versions, we should have an idea of the outline of each in order to avoid confusion. Luke purposefully rearranges the outline of Mark (which Matthew follows), and part of the purpose of this chapter is to determine why. However, despite different placement of events in the two outlines, the development of each segment within each section is more or less parallel in the three accounts.

Outline

MATTHEW AND MARK	**LUKE**
A. Introduction: Jesus taken to the high priest's; Peter sitting by the fire.	A. Introduction: Jesus taken to the high priest's; Peter sitting by the fire
B. Night trial	B. Peter's denials and repentance
C. Mockery and beating	C. Mockery and beating
D. Peter's denials and repentance	D. Morning trial

One of the reasons for Luke's placement of the trial in the morning was that night trials were illegal according to Jewish law, and scrupulous adherents to the Law like these elders would certainly have avoided that. Perhaps Mark and Matthew place it at night to underline the perversion of justice in condemning Jesus, even though Luke's placement is probably more historical. But the injustice of the trial, because of the obvious rigging of evidence and obvious perjury, would have been clear whether the trial had been held at night or at noon. But Luke also has a further, subtler reason for his order, as we will see.

Therefore, the reader should remember that, although the trial segments and the denial segments are printed in parallel lines for purposes of step-by-step comparison in the three versions, the overall placement in Luke is purposefully different from Mark's and Matthew's structure.

The Sanhedrin was a group of 71 chief priests, elders, and scribes along with the ruling high priest of the year. They decided religious, legal, and internal civic matters for Jews—anything that did not pertain to the Roman law. In judicial processes, defense witnesses were called first and then prosecution witnesses; notice that no defense witnesses are called in any of the three versions.

A. Introduction

MATTHEW 26
⁵⁷Then those who had seized Jesus led him to Caiaphas, the high priest, where the scribes and the elders had gathered.

MARK 14
⁵³And they led Jesus to the high priest; and all the chief priests and the elders and the scribes were assembled.

LUKE 22
⁵⁴Then they seized him and led him away, bringing him into the high priest's house.

⁵⁸But Peter followed him at a distance, as far as the courtyard of the high priest, and going inside he sat with the guards to see the end.

And Peter had followed him at a distance, right into the courtyard of the high priest; and he was sitting with the guards and warming himself at the fire.

Peter followed at a distance; ⁵⁵and when they had kindled a fire in the middle of the courtyard and sat down together, Peter sat among them.

Unraveling the Meaning

- Notice all the "ands" in Mark's version, and that he does not say who "they" are. What does "right into the courtyard" tell about his style? Yet Mark does add the homey detail about Peter warming himself at the fire which Matthew, for some reason, omits.

- Why would Matthew have been more likely to know the name of the high priest for that year than Mark or Luke?

MARK'S simplicity of style is clear (especially if one looks at this passage with the one immediately preceding) by the succession of compound sentences: "and . . . and . . . and." There are hardly any complex sentences or subordinate clauses. But the toughness of his style comes through in that cocky "right into the courtyard."

MATTHEW follows Mark very closely, adding only the grim note "to see the end."

LUKE also follows Mark closely, although he omits naming the members of the court at this time, holding off until he comes to the trial the next morning. His focus for the moment is not on the trial but on Peter, whom he shows denying Jesus before the trial rather than after it.

The following segment is long. Read Mark through first, then section by section compare Mark and Matthew, then section by section compare Luke with both.

B. The Trial (D, in Luke)

MATTHEW 26

MARK 14

LUKE 22

66When day came, the assembly of the elders of the people gathered together, both chief priests and scribes; and they led him away to their council,

59Now the chief priests and the whole council sought false testimony against Jesus that they might put him to death, 60but they found none, though many false witnesses came forward.

55Now the chief priests and the whole council sought testimony against Jesus to put him to death; but they found none. 56For many bore false witness against him, and their witness did not agree.

At last two came forward 61and said, "This fellow said 'I am able to destroy the temple of God, and to build it in three days.'"

57And some stood up and bore false witness against him, saying, "We heard him say, 'I will destroy this temple that is made with hands, and in three days I will build another not made with hands.'"

62And the high priest stood up and said "Have you no answer

59Yet not even so did their testimony agree. 60And the high priest

to make? What is it
that these men testify
against you?" But
Jesus was silent.

stood up in the midst,
and asked Jesus,
"Have you no answer
to make? What is it
that these men testify
against you?"
[61]But he was silent
and made no answer.

And the high priest
said to him, "I adjure
you by the living God,
tell us if you are the
Christ, the Son of
God."

Again the high priest
asked him,
"Are you the Christ,
the Son of the
Blessed?"

and they said,
[67]If you are the Christ,
tell us." But he said to
them, "If I tell you, you
will not believe; [68]and
if I ask you, you will
not answer.

[64]Jesus said to him,
"You have said so. But
I tell you, hereafter
you will see the Son
of man seated at the
right hand of Power,
and coming on the
clouds of heaven."

[62]And Jesus said, "I
am; and you will see
the Son of man sitting
at the right hand of
Power, and coming
with the clouds of
heaven."

[69] "But from now on
the Son of man will be
seated at the right
hand of the power of
God."
[70]And they all said,
"Are you the Son of
God, then?" And he
said to them, "You say
that I am."

[65]The high priest tore
his robes, and said,
"He has uttered
blasphemy. Why do
we still need
witnesses? You have
now heard his
blasphemy. [66]What is
your judgment?" They
answered, "He
deserves death.

[63]And the high priest
tore his mantle, and
said, "Why do we still
need witnesses? [64]You
have heard his
blasphemy. What is
your decision?" And
they all condemned
him as deserving
death.

[71]And they said,
"What further
testimony do we
need? We have heard
it ourselves from his
own lips."

Unraveling the Meaning

- What words in Mark and Matthew show that the result of the trial is a foregone conclusion?

- Look for ways that Matthew has "cleaned up" Mark's style.

- How does the reader know that the charge about the Temple is false? Matthew's version is "cleaner," but how is Mark's closer to Jesus' actual statement on that topic?

- Why does Matthew omit "and made no answer"?

- Why does Luke omit all reference to trumped up charges and false witnesses? How do his verses 67–68 do the same job?

- Why is the high priest's question illegal—in any court?

- Both Matthew and Luke change Mark's version of Jesus' answer to the high priest. Why?

- What does tearing one's clothes mean in such a situation? Why would Luke, writing for Gentiles, omit it?

MARK: Although it is clear in both Mark and Matthew that the priests had made up their minds beforehand about the outcome of the trial, Mark repeats "false witnesses" in both vv. 56 and 57, hammering it home.

Mark alone specifies the temple made with hands and the temple not made with hands. Symbolically, the first temple means Israel, focused as it was in the Temple at Jerusalem; the second temple is the new church of Christ, the body in which his Spirit would continue to dwell. (It should be noted that Mark was writing his narrative long after the historical events he records, and he was therefore influenced by his knowledge of the very real antagonism between the "two temples" in his own day.)

In contrast to the other two synoptics, Jesus gives a clear affirmative answer in Mark's version to the high priest's questions about his being the Christ: "I am." These words, of course, are a formula most Jews avoided, since it was the way Yahweh had identified himself to Moses. To this day, orthodox Jews will not even write the word "God" but rather "G-d." Yahweh's name—"I am"—was unspeakable, so that when asked a question like "Are you the culprit?" or "Are you called Simon?," a good Jew would use a circumlocution like, "You have said it," or "As you say." (Recall that in John's version of the arrest, when Jesus says, "I am," the Jews fall on the ground in shock at this blasphemous self-assertion.)

Note, too, that in having Jesus' own vigorous admission of who he is at this point, Peter's later denial of who he himself is becomes even more cowardly by contrast. Jesus stands up to the chiefs of his nation, but Peter buckles before maids and bystanders.

In both Mark and Matthew, the high priest recognizes only too well the seemingly blasphemous assertion Jesus makes of himself as well as the obvious reference to the Son of Man.

MATTHEW gives the name "Caiaphas," and only Matthew has him put Jesus under oath to answer. This surely underlines the injustice, since it asks the defendant under oath to incriminate himself. While Mark's false witnesses quote Jesus as saying "I will destroy the temple," Matthew softens it to "I am able to." This is interesting, especially since most scholars agree that Mark wrote before the actual destruction of the Temple and Matthew wrote after.

Although Matthew, the good Hebrew mind, avoids the "I am" by using "You have said so," the rest of the verse leaves no doubt what Jesus was claiming. And, as in Mark, the horror of the high priest underlines that. For those people of our own day who admire Jesus as "a wonderful model, like Mohandas Gandhi," the testimony of this Jewish high priest shows that Jesus himself made a claim far more dramatic than mere moral leadership. There's an irony there somewhere.

LUKE'S order begins to show advantages regarding Peter. Whereas Mark and Matthew show Peter "topping things off" by deserting Jesus even when he supposedly knows the trial Jesus has endured, Luke has his denials before the bitter experience of the trial.

The most notable thing in Luke's description of the trial is that there are no accusations, no witnesses, no mention of blasphemy, no condemnation. Even the identity of the speakers is left as an indefinite "they." The question is: Who are you? It could be a moment from *Oedipus the King*.

Recall, too, the description of the arrest in Luke: This is the critical moment, the fullness of time. This question— "Who are you?"—has been hounding Jesus throughout Luke's gospel, from the three temptations in the desert right up to the three taunting temptations from the bystanders at the cross. "Who are you?" "If you are the Son of God, throw yourself off the Temple and you will be saved; if you are the Son of God, come down from the cross." In the answer to the questions of Jesus' identity, Luke changes the order of the three titles of Mark-Matthew: Christ . . . Son of God (the Blessed) . . . Son of man.

Moreover, unlike Mark and Matthew who say the Jews "will" see Jesus coming as the Son of man in divine power on the clouds (at the end of the world), Luke says "from now on" the Son of man will be seated on a par with the divine power.

Luke is not looking so much to the Kingdom's fulfillment in the end but at its present and growing reality in the Christian community. The kingdom is about to begin; and as Luke writes, Jesus is already glorified.

In the passage which follows, remember that in Luke's version the mockery comes before Jesus' actual trial (in the morning), whereas in Mark and Matthew it comes as a "natural" result of the condemnation.

C. The Mocking

MATTHEW 26
⁶⁷Then they spat in his face, and struck him; and some slapped him, saying, "Prophesy to us, you Christ! Who is it that struck you?"

MARK 14
⁶⁵And some began to spit on him, and to cover his face, and to strike him, saying to him "Prophesy!" And the guards received him with blows.

LUKE 22
⁶³Now the men who were holding Jesus mocked him and beat him; ⁶⁴they also blind-folded him and asked him, "Prophesy! Who is it that struck you?" ⁶⁵And they spoke many other words against him, reviling him.

Unraveling the Meaning

- Mark begins this segment immediately after the condemnation at the trial. In the second verse, "the guards received him with blows." What does that imply about the persons spitting on Jesus and striking him in the previous verse?

- How does Luke clarify that? What does Luke, typically, omit from Mark's version?

MARK shows Jesus being mocked first, and only then does he seem to be turned over to the guards who, apparently in their turn, received him and began beating him. This would imply that the initial tormentors were the people spoken of immediately before this in Mark's gospel: the priests and elders.

MATTHEW dodges the ambiguity by omitting reference to the guards. In Mark and Luke the "game" is apparently to blindfold their Victim and, since he is a prophet, dare him to say which of them had hit him that time. Matthew, who is usually cautious about such matters, neglects to tell us that the blindfold was put on.

LUKE, with typical delicacy, spares us the indignity of even suspecting priests guilty of such loathsomeness by saying that it was "the men who were holding Jesus." Nor does he say anything about "spittle," preferring to hide something so disgusting under a vague phrase like "many other words" and "reviling."

D. Peter's Denials and Repentance (B, in Luke)

MATTHEW 26	**MARK 14**	**LUKE 22**
⁶⁹Now Peter was sitting outside in the courtyard. And a maid	⁶⁶And as Peter was below in the courtyard, one of the	⁵⁶Then a maid, seeing him as he sat in the light and gazing at

came up to him, and said, "You also were with Jesus the Galilean." [70]But he denied it before them all, saying, "I do not know what you mean."

[71]And when he went out to the porch, another maid saw him, and she said to the bystanders, "This man was with Jesus of Nazareth." [72]And again he denied it with an oath, "I do not know the man."

[73]After a little while the bystanders came up and said to Peter, "Certainly you are also one of them, for your accent betrays you." [74]Then he began to invoke a curse on himself and to swear, "I do not know the man." And immediately the cock crowed.

[75]And Peter remembered the saying of Jesus, "Before the cock crows, you will

maids of the high priest came; [67]and seeing Peter warming himself, she looked at him, and said, "You also were with the Nazarene, Jesus." [68]But he denied it, saying, "I neither know nor understand what you mean."

And he went out into the gateway. [69]And the maid saw him, and began again to say to the bystanders, "This man is one of them." [70]But again he denied it.

And after a little while again the bystanders said to Peter, "Certainly you are one of them; for you are a Galilean." [71]But he began to invoke a curse on himself and to swear, "I do not know this man of whom you speak." [72]And immediately the cock crowed a second time.

And Peter remembered how Jesus had said to him, "Before the cock crows twice,

him, said, "This man also was with him." [57]But he denied it, saying, "Woman, I do not know him."

[58]And a little later some one else saw him and said, "You also are one of them." But Peter said, "Man I am not!"

[59]And after an interval of about an hour still another insisted, saying "Certainly this man also was with him; for he is a Galilean." [60]But Peter said, "Man, I do not know what you are saying." And immediately, while he was still speaking, the cock crowed.

[61]And the Lord turned and looked at Peter. And Peter remembered the word of the

deny me three times." | you will deny me | Lord, how he had said
And he went out and | three times." And he | to him, "Before the
wept bitterly. | broke down and wept. | cock crows today, you
| | will deny me three
| | times."
| | [62]And he went out and
| | wept bitterly

Unraveling the Meaning

- In what ways do Matthew and Luke "tighten up" Mark?

- How is it more likely that, as in Matthew and Luke, it would not be the same maid the second time, as in Mark?

- In Mark and Luke the woman knows Peter is a Galilean, but only Matthew gives the reason. What is it?

- In v. 72, Mark says the cock crowed a second time. What is odd about that?

- Luke says "the Lord turned and looked at Peter." How is that possible?

MARK: Notice how Mark makes a typical careless "Markism" when the cock crows for the second time, and Mark has not bothered to tell us it crowed the first time! A touch of Greek makes the end of Mark's version of the scene more vital. *Epibalon eklaien* can better be translated, "He threw himself down and wept and wept."

MATTHEW builds a climax better than Mark. In his version Peter is accosted first by one maid, then another, then by all the bystanders. And it is only Matthew who gives a legitimate reason why the bystanders would immediately know Peter was not a native of Jerusalem. (This segment, among many other reasons, convinces scholars that although both Matthew and Luke knew Mark's version and used it, neither knew of the other's version. This dramatic buildup and the concrete reason for unmasking Peter would have appealed to Luke, and had he known of Matthew's version, he surely would have used it.)

LUKE, again with his delicate concern for both Peter and Jesus, says nothing about swearing. He also heightens the dramatic impact of the scene's climax by having the cock crow, "while he was still speaking."

But the most memorable detail that Luke inserts is the chilling: "And the Lord turned and looked at Peter." Whether Jesus actually was being brought by at that moment (in Luke's version on his way to the morning trial) or not is hardly important. Luke has far more meaningful things to do than concentrate on accurate reportage.

Recall the passage, in Luke only, at the Last Supper: "Simon, Simon, behold, Satan demanded to have you, that he might sift you like wheat, but I have prayed for you that your faith may not fail; and *when you have turned again,* strengthen your brethren" (Luke 22:31–32). Immediately, Peter began to defend himself and swear he would go to prison and even death with Jesus. At that moment, Luke says Jesus predicted this triple denial before the cock crowed. When the event occurs in the courtyard, Jesus "turns" to Peter and Peter "turns" back to Jesus.

The Hebrew word for "conversion"—like the Latin and Greek words for "conversion"—is the word "to turn back," to get back to the right way of doing things. It is consistent in both Isaiah (in Hebrew) and Luke (in Greek) that the Lord must first turn toward us *(strephein,* like the Latin *vertere,* "turn") before we can turn back toward him *(epistraphein,* like the Latin *convertere,* "return").

Throughout his gospel, Luke has made a special effort to picture Peter as the "model disciple," a mixture of belief and fear, relying on the Lord and coming back to begin over even after he has sinned.

Just as Peter is the focal character of Luke's gospel, Paul is the focal character of Luke's Acts. Both are "converts" in this two-volume work of Luke—Peter with this shattering experience in the courtyard, Paul with his shattering experience on the road to Damascus. In both cases, the Lord turns first and they, with awesome realization, turn wholly to him.

It is somewhat easier now to see why Luke might have put this scene *before* Jesus' trial rather than after it. This event surely deprives Jesus of his last friend, but—like the mother in labor—Jesus knows that this pain from Peter and the pain to come will bear fruit when the Kingdom is born.

Summary of Different Emphases

MARK

Mark is typically assertive: Jesus says forthrightly, "I am," even at the risk of confounding Jews who would never use those words. As is common with Mark, the Good News is meant to shock. Nor does he shy away from showing his friend, Peter, the first pope, denying with oaths that he even knew Jesus—within hours of his own first communion, his ordination as a priest, and his first Mass. It was not an easy-going, one-hour-a-week Christian community Mark was writing for; they were under threat at every minute from Roman prisons and martyrdom.

Even the first pope gave in to the enemy. But he was forgiven, and he died a martyr only a year or two before Mark's gospel was written and in the very city where his gospel circulated.

MATTHEW

In this segment, too, Matthew's Jewish training and sensibilities come through. He knows the name of the high priest, he knows the need of witnesses, but he does not hesitate to underline the illegality of the trial by putting it at night and showing no defense witnesses were allowed. Like any other Jew, he hesitates to use "I am," the name of God, and like any other Jew, he draws back from picturing the chief priests spitting at Jesus and striking him—which Mark finds not difficult at all.

LUKE

Luke's version of the trial is the barest: there are no accusations, no witnesses, no mention of blasphemy, no condemnation. The whole thing hinges on who Jesus is. When he answers that question, the trial is over. Unlike Matthew and Mark, Luke does not see Jesus in the apocalyptic terms of Daniel, coming to power only in the end time. "From now on" the Son of Man will share the power of Yahweh. Also, for Luke's audience the Roman trial was probably the only important, "official" one.

But the most striking difference in Luke is his switching of the trial and Peter's denials from Mark's original order. In the first place, Luke's ordering of events evades the obvious illegality of a night trial, which the elders would probably not have risked with a person they wanted to get out of the way as much as they did Jesus. The temper of the people who had greeted Jesus with hosannahs the previous Sunday was too volatile for that.

Secondly, the "desertion" by Peter leaves Jesus more dramatically abandoned at the beginning of the trial. This most ardent disciple—with whom the weak Christian reader can so easily identify—allows the reader to "get into Peter's shoes" and see what abandoning Jesus is like. Moreover, Peter's denials are given so much stress in homilies that it is easy to forget that, for all his bluster and failings, Peter was at least not hiding out with the others in the upper room. He failed the test in the courtyard, but at least he was courageous (or foolhardy) enough not to run away from the test as the others had done.

Finally, with his customary kindness, Luke disassociates Peter from "the bad guys" by having not only his denial but his conversion occur before the mockery of Jesus by his captors and the travesty of justice at his trial. However, Luke's version is still a slower and more literary stripping-away of one support after another from Jesus—as one finds in Greek drama.

Summary of Similarities

Although Luke purposefully reverses the Peter section and the trial section, the development of events within each section is relatively the same.

Although in Luke the outcome of the trial is not as explicitly a foregone conclusion and although there are no false witnesses, the pivotal question is whether Jesus is the Christ. In all three, Jesus says that he is. When he does that, the trial is over.

In all three gospels, there is an intentional and bitter irony of situation: Jesus, who is regal in his ability to rise up above his treatment, is on trial on precisely those grounds: his kingship. And his condemnation is at the hands of leaders and priests, who condemn him in the name of God.

In all three, even in Luke who shies from such ugliness, Jesus is mocked, beaten and told to prophesy.

All four evangelists, even John, agree that Peter's denials occurred at night. He is challenged three times and each time renounces his faith in Jesus publicly. The cock crows, he remembers Jesus' warning, and he repents with bitter tears.

Jesus' silence in this trial and in the trial with Pilate has two purposes. First, at the time the gospels were written, all communications between the Jewish community and the Christian community had broken down. Orthodox Jews were even turning Christians into the civil authorities as members of a new religion that perverted true Judaism—which the Romans tolerated. In these trials, there is an example of that breakdown in communications right from the start, as well as an example to those who themselves were to be handed over by their fellow Jews to the Roman authorities and condemned to death. Jesus' silence shows how the first Christians reacted to a trial which many of the first readers of these gospels would themselves be called to undergo.

Secondly, though, Jesus' silence was also the will of God, expressed to him and to the Jewish nation in prophecies about how Yahweh would treat his anointed: "Harshly dealt with, he bore it humbly; he never opened his mouth, like a lamb that is led to the slaughterhouse; like a sheep that is dumb before its shearers, never opening its mouth." Isaiah 53 is only one of many passages like this, but it is worth reading as a foreshadowing of this most critical weekend in the life of humankind.

Chapter Eleven

THE ROMAN TRIAL

As in the Jewish trial, all three evangelists telescope events in the trial before Pilate. Any dramatic presentation of a trial does the same thing (e.g., *Perry Mason)*. We are spared such details as jury selection, swearing in, etc., in order to focus on the more important aspects of the proceedings, especially the climax. Here, too, the important factor is not details of the process but the pressures that determined the outcome: the tensions Pilate faced with Jesus' evident innocence on the one side and the Jewish leaders' threatening insistence on the other.

The outlines are again parallel, but there are insertions by Matthew and Luke and a different structuring of the materials within the segments; all of these changes from Mark's outline are purposeful. (And notice that Mark wraps up the episode in 15 verses, where Matthew gives it 26 verses and Luke gives it 24 verses.)

Outline

MATTHEW	MARK	LUKE
A. Morning; Jesus to Pilate	A. Morning; Jesus to Pilate	A. Morning; Jesus to Pilate
B. Death of Judas		B. Charge of treason
C. Jesus questioned	C. Jesus questioned	C. Jesus questioned; declared innocent; repetition of treason.
		D. Jesus to Herod; declared innocent; repetition of treason

E. Offer of Barabbas; Pilate's wife's dream	E. Offer of Barabbas	
F. Choice of Barabbas	F. Choice of Barabbas	F. Choice of Barabbas
G. "Crucify him!"	G. "Crucify him!"	G. "Crucify him!"
H. Pilate's hand washing		
I. Barabbas released; Jesus handed over.	I. Barabbas released; Jesus handed over.	I. Barabbas released; Jesus handed over.

A. Morning: Jesus Sent to Pilate

MATTHEW 27	MARK 15	LUKE 23
¹When morning came, all the chief priests and the elders of the people took counsel against Jesus to put him to death; ²and they bound him and led him away	¹And as soon as it was morning the chief priests, with the elders and scribes, and the whole council held a consultation; and they bound Jesus and led him away	
and delivered him to Pilate the governor.	and delivered him to Pilate.	¹Then the whole company of them arose, and brought him before Pilate.

Mark and Matthew make some small attempt to put a touch of legality on the proceedings by having this morning "consultation." Even though the actual trial had been, illegally, at night, the official decision was made in the morning. Luke, who has put the trial itself in the morning, simply goes on to the next step. Note again how Mark very simply strings events together with no other transition word but "and."

B. The Death of Judas (Matthew only)

MATTHEW 27

³When Judas, his betrayer, saw that he was condemned, he repented and brought back the thirty pieces of silver to the chief priests and the elders, ⁴saying, "I have sinned in betraying innocent blood." They said, "What is that to us? See to it yourself." ⁵And throwing down the pieces of silver in the temple, he departed; and he went and hanged himself. ⁶But the chief priests, taking the pieces of silver, said, "It is not lawful to put them into the treasury since they are blood money." ⁷So they took counsel, and bought with them the potter's field, to bury strangers in. ⁸Therefore, that field has been called the Field of Blood to this day. ⁹Then was fulfilled what had been spoken by the prophet Jeremiah, saying, "And they took the thirty pieces of silver, the price of him on whom a price had been set by some of the sons of Israel, ¹⁰and they gave them for the potter's field, as the Lord directed me."

Unraveling the Meaning

- Just as Peter had, Judas "repented." What is the core difference between the two?

- The death of Judas seems almost peripheral in this insertion. But two other items are mentioned again and again. Which two? Why?

- Considering Matthew's radical purpose in converting Jews to accept the Messiah, what motive is he working on here?

- This event cannot possibly be in chronological sequence. Why not?

MATTHEW: The emphasis is not on the death of Judas but rather on the silver (used four times itself and referred to by "it" three times) and on the price of blood (three times).

Why insert it here, since it can't possibly be in chronological sequence: How can the chief priests be with Pilate and with Judas at the same time? Judas didn't meet them "along the way"; the episode explicitly takes place in the Temple.

There most probably was a "potter's field" (the better translation is probably "treasury's field") near Jerusalem where strangers were buried called "The Field of Blood." Matthew has a far larger purpose here than a historical process of tracing the name of a burial plot back to the time of Jesus.

For Matthew, the insistence on "the price of blood" emphasizes the whole tone of these trials. When Pilate washes his hands of the case—only in Matthew (27:25), the Jews call out that grisly challenge, "His blood be on us and on our children!" That sentence is the whole point of the scene, and Matthew, who is not writing history but trying to explain it, inserts this episode of Judas to put the event of Jesus' condemnation in the full perspective of history. The Jewish leaders, like Judas, have the blood of an innocent man on their hands. But Judas and then Pilate refuse to continue the responsibility for such an injustice, leaving the Jews alone to carry the burden—which they willingly do, according to Matthew.

On the other hand, no matter what the guilt of the Jewish leaders who incite the crowds to ask for Barabbas and call for Jesus' death, they cannot overturn the plan of Jesus and his

Father revealed throughout Jewish history. Just as Judas is a pawn in the hands of the Jewish leaders, the leaders themselves are pawns in the hands of the Enemy—who, in turn, is a pawn in the hands of God. Their very act of "buying God" with blood money was predicted by the prophet Zechariah (not Jeremiah): "But God told me, 'Throw into the treasury this princely sum at which they have valued me.' Taking the 30 shekels of silver, I threw them into the Temple of Yahweh" (Zechariah 11:13). Matthew was doubtless quoting from memory.

Did Zechariah foresee Judas photographically? Or is Matthew recording a historical event? Very likely not. But both did know the ways of Yahweh, and Yahweh was preparing Israel for its Messiah. Matthew (or his sources) knew of (1) the passage in Zechariah, (2) the betrayal of the Messiah by Judas—and by the Jewish leaders, (3) most important, the meaning of this event in the light of God's dealings with God's people over the ages.

C. Jesus is Questioned

MATTHEW 27	MARK 15	LUKE 23
		[2]And they began to accuse him, saying, "We found this man perverting our nation, and forbidding us to give tribute to Caesar, and saying that he himself is Christ a king."

¹¹Now Jesus stood before the governor; and the governor asked him, "Are you the King of the Jews?" Jesus said to him, "You have said so."

²And Pilate asked him, "Are you the King of the Jews?" And he answered him, "You have said so."

¹²But when he was accused by the chief priests and elders, he made no answer. ¹³Then Pilate said to him, "Do you not hear how many things they testify against you?" ¹⁴But he gave them no answer, not even to a single charge; so that the governor wondered greatly.

³And the chief priests accused him of many things.
⁴And Pilate again asked him, "Have you no answer to make? See how many charges they bring against you." ⁵But Jesus made no further answer, so that Pilate wondered.

⁴And Pilate said to the chief priests and the multitudes, "I find no crime in this man."
⁵But they were urgent, saying, "He stirs up the people, teaching throughout all Judea, from Galilee even to this place."

Unraveling the Meaning

- In the passion accounts of the Sanhedrin trial, was there any mention of "forbidding us to give tribute to Caesar"? Roman law said that a conquered people could not resort to the death penalty. Why has the charge been changed? Matthew and Mark will get around to this drastic change in the charges against Jesus, but why does Luke—considering his audience—insert it right at the top of the scene?

- How can you tell, from Pilate's first question to Jesus, that the evangelists have omitted a great deal? How does Jesus' response to Pilate in Mark differ from his answer to a similar question from the high priest? What is the difference between being "the Son of the Most High" and being "King of the Jews"?

- Even allowing for "telescoping," is there any justification for Luke jumping from the accusation to Pilate's immediate declaration that Jesus is innocent?

- Why is Jesus silent?

MARK (and Matthew) start off slam-bang in the middle of the trial, without even an accusation to Pilate. Mark, writing for Romans, didn't need to mention who Pilate was or what his office was. But the Jews deliver Jesus, and right away Pilate asks, "Are you the King of the Jews?"—which incidentally had been no part of the previous evening's accusations. Once Jesus admits (with the Jewish avoidance of "I am") that he is indeed the King of the Jews, the chief priests accuse him of "many things." The whole thing is a charade anyway, and Mark wants to get it over with. The pagan Pilate wonders, but the Jews—despite their knowledge of their Scripture—do not.

MATTHEW constantly stresses that Pilate is the governor (four times already in the chapter). Other than that he has a remarkable similarity to Mark.

LUKE, throughout the Roman trial, has a clearer-cut structure. Alone of the three evangelists, Luke has the accusation loud and clear before Pilate asks any questions: The charge is not blasphemy, but treason. Despite what Jesus himself had preached (Luke 20:25 and parallels) about rendering to Caesar the things that are Caesar's, they charge him with forbidding Jews to give tribute. This further underlines the deceitfulness of the chief priests. But it also stands out in stark contrast to Pilate's official declaration: "I find no crime in this man," which he will repeat three more times before Luke's treatment of the scene is over. (Remember, too, that Luke is writing for a Gentile audience.) But despite Pilate's judgment, the priests and the "multitudes" shout again that Jesus is a political revolutionary and has been stirring up all Judea, from a base in Galilee, where guerrillas often trained and hid out.

Only in Luke, the reference to Galilee, which was under the jurisdiction of the puppet Jewish king, Herod, gives Pilate what he thinks may be an "out."

D. Jesus Is Sent to Herod (Luke only)

LUKE 23

⁶When Pilate heard this, he asked whether the man was a Galilean. ⁷And when he learned that he belonged to Herod's jurisdiction, he sent him over to Herod, who was himself in Jerusalem at that time. ⁸When Herod saw Jesus, he was very glad, for he had long desired to see him, because he had heard about him, and he was hoping to see some sign done by him. ⁹So he questioned him at some length; but he made no answer. ¹⁰The chief priests and the scribes stood by, vehemently accusing him. ¹¹And Herod with his soldiers treated him with contempt and mocked him; then,

arraying him in gorgeous apparel, he sent him back to Pilate. [12]And Herod and Pilate became friends with each other that very day, for before this they had been at enmity with each other.

Unraveling the Meaning

- Herod was a petty king, used by the Romans as a figurehead. What was his probable reaction to this recognition of his "jurisdiction"? How does Herod treat Jesus, someone who is also a believing Jew?

- How is Jesus' silence beginning to "bellow"?

- Luke has softened the mockery of the Roman soldiers but here inserts a mockery by Jews. Why?

- If you can explain "Herod and Pilate became friends," you can probably get a post at the Biblicum seminary in Rome.

LUKE: Galilee had been a staging area for guerilla uprisings for a long time, as such barren hill country so frequently is for occupied peoples. Herod, the puppet king of Galilee, is mentioned only once in Matthew and only twice in Mark, but six times in Luke's gospel and twice in Luke's Acts of the Apostles.

This is the same Herod who beheaded John the Baptist and who, some Pharisees told Jesus, was trying to kill Jesus, too. He is the same Herod whom Jesus called "that fox."

Two of Luke's references may indicate his sources for this and other details about Herod. In Acts 13:1, he mentions Manaen, an elder of the church in Antioch who had grown up with Herod; some scholars suspect that Luke may have written in Antioch. In Luke 8:3, he mentions Joanna, the wife of Chuza who was Herod's steward; only Luke mentions that this Joanna was one of the women who followed Jesus and was at his tomb. Either or both of these people could have been the source of this episode in Luke, which the other two evangelists seem to have been unaware of.

Why does Luke insert it here? For one reason, it might very well be historical. For another, it emphasizes still further the Gentile Pilate's attempts to avoid condemning Jesus—by flattering Herod into declaring a stay of execution. Remember, too, that Luke's readers had never heard this story before, and as a storyteller, Luke knew this possibility of the hero finding a way out would increase the suspense, especially since the hero is so manifestly innocent.

Mark later has the Roman soldiers put a mock king-costume on Jesus, and Luke here has the Jewish king do that.

Furthermore, this Herod seems very well caricatured in *Jesus Christ Superstar*—an overindulged Eastern monarch looking for diversion, a magic trick, from this reputed miracle worker. Like his people, he is asking for a "sign" and doesn't see that Jesus is the sign of the Suffering Servant of Yahweh, standing right in front of him.

While Jesus responds to Pilate's questions, he is completely silent here. According to the Book of Wisdom (8:12), even the powerful must wait for a wise man in his silence. Sirach 20:1 says that the wise man remains silent in the face of rebuke that is uncalled for, while the fool "multiplies words." (The Roman writer Martial put it more clearly: "There is no glory in excelling a jackass.")

At any rate, Herod cannot condemn Jesus and sends him back to Pilate, who also cannot condemn him. Luke thus has his biblical requirement of two witnesses, officially testifying to Jesus' innocence.

"Herod and Pilate became friends." Apparently there had been a feud between them, and perhaps Herod takes this recognition of his petty authority as a kind of peace offering from Pilate—which is ironic, considering that Pilate was trying to get rid of a hot potato.

Later in Acts, Luke tells of the prayer offered by the community after the elders of the synagogue had released Peter and John. They begin quoting Genesis and draw a conclusion about Jerusalem, Herod, and Pilate:

"'Kings on earth setting out to war, princes making an alliance, against the Lord and against his anointed.' This is what has come true: in this very city Herod and Pontius Pilate *made an alliance* between the pagan *nations* and the *peoples* of Israel, against your holy servant Jesus, whom you *anointed,* but only to bring about the very thing that you in your strength and wisdom had predetermined should happen" (Acts 4:26-29).

E. The Sentence of Death

MATTHEW 27	MARK 15	LUKE 23
		[13]Pilate then called together the chief priests and the rulers and the people, [14]and said to them, "You brought me this man as one who was perverting the people; and after examining him before you, behold, I did not find this man guilty of any of your charges

against him; ¹⁵neither did Herod, for he sent him back to us. Behold, nothing deserving death has been done by him; ¹⁶I will therefore chastise him and release him."

¹⁵Now at the feast the governor was accustomed to release for the crowd any one prisoner whom they wanted.

⁶Now at the feast he used to release for them one prisoner whom they asked.

¹⁶And they had then a notorious prisoner, called Barabbas. ¹⁷So when they had gathered, Pilate said to them, "Whom do you want me to release for you, Barabbas or Jesus who is called Christ?" ¹⁸For he knew that it was out of envy that they had delivered him up.

⁷And among the rebels in prison, who had committed murder in the insurrection, there was a man called Barabbas. ⁸And the crowd came up and began to ask Pilate to do as he was wont to do for them. ⁹And he answered them, "Do you want me to release for you the King of the Jews?" ¹⁰For he perceived that it was out of envy that the chief priests had delivered him up.

¹⁹Besides, while he was sitting on the judgment seat, his wife sent word to him, "Have nothing to do with that righteous

man, for I have suffered much over him today in a dream."

20Now the chief priests and the elders persuaded the people to ask for Barabbas and destroy Jesus. 21The governor again said to them, "Which of the two do you want me to release for you?" And they said, "Barabbas." 22Pilate said to them, "Then what shall I do with Jesus who is called Christ?"

11But the chief priests stirred up the crowd to have him release for them Barabbas instead. 12And Pilate again said to them, "Then what shall I do with the man whom you call the King of the Jews?"

18But they all cried out together. "Away with this man, and release to us Barabbas"—19a man who had been thrown into prison for an insurrection started in the city, and for murder. 20Pilate addressed them once more, desiring to release Jesus;

They all said, "Let him be crucified." 23And he said, "Why? What evil has he done?" But they shouted all the more, "Let him be crucified." 24So when Pilate saw that he was gaining nothing, but rather that a riot was beginning, he took water and washed his hands before the crowd, saying ,"I am innocent of this righteous man's blood, see to it your-selves." 25And all the people answered, "His

13And they cried out again, "Crucify him." 14And Pilate said to them, "Why? What evil has he done?" But they shouted all the more, "Crucify him."

21but they shouted out, "Crucify, crucify him!" 22A third time he said to them, "Why? What evil has he done?" I have found in him no crime deserving death; I will therefore chastise him and release him." But they were urgent, demanding with loud cries that he should be crucified. And their voices prevailed.

blood be on us and on our children!"

²⁶Then he released for them Barabbas, and having scourged Jesus, delivered him to be crucified.

¹⁵So Pilate, wishing to satisfy the crowd, released for them Barabbas; and having scourged Jesus, he delivered him to be crucified.

²⁴So Pilate gave sentence that their demand should be granted. ²⁵He released the man who had been thrown into prison for insurrection and murder, whom they asked for; but Jesus he delivered up to their will.

Unraveling the Meaning

- How many times does Luke show Pilate saying that Jesus is innocent? Why?

- The name Barabbas comes from "bar" (son of) and "abba" (father). Why is it ironic that Jesus is offered in exchange for "the son of the father"? Barabbas has been a convicted murderer and insurrectionist; how does his crime compare to Jesus'? Mark calls Jesus "King of the Jews." Why does Matthew change it?

- What dramatic purpose is served in Matthew by inserting the story about Pilate's wife's dream? How does it show that Luke was unaware of Matthew's version when he wrote his?

- Only Matthew has shown Judas repenting of Jesus' blood, and only he shows Pilate washing his hands—

and explicitly says washing them of Jesus' blood. Why is Matthew pushing this?

MARK is again expeditious. Pilate has a very small role here, in contrast to the uses both Matthew and Luke put him to. Perceiving the elders' envious motives, he offers them Jesus as his regular Passover amnesty. He argues when they ask for Barabbas, but they shout him down and—crowd-pleaser as Mark sees him—he gives in.

MATTHEW follows Mark's text except for three dramatic liberties.

Most critics agree that the intervention of Pilate's wife and her dream are a legend Matthew has heard about the trial, one he uses to dramatic effect, offering Pilate one more motive for interfering in the priests' plans. (According to the Jewish historian Josephus, the historical Pilate was surely not a man renowned for kindliness and caution!) Matthew also has used dreams in his infancy narratives.

Pilate's symbolic handwashing is another way of under-lining this man's "innocence" and therefore the treachery of the Jewish leaders. And it also fits the pattern Matthew has set up with the thirty pieces of silver being the price of this man's blood. Matthew has used this reference to shedding the blood of the prophets before, in the woes Jesus has called down on the scribes and Pharisees earlier:

> "Alas for you, scribes and Pharisees, you hypocrites! You who build sepulchres of the prophets and decorate the tombs of holy men, saying, 'We would never have joined in shedding the blood of the prophets, had we lived in our fathers' day.' So! Your own evidence tells against you! You are the sons of those who murdered the prophets! Very well, then, finish off the work that your fathers began."
>
> (Matthew 23:29–32)

The manner in which the Jews—and Matthew is careful to say "*all* the people"—call this blood down on themselves and on their children is chilling. It is ironic that at this Passover, which celebrated the feast whereby the Israelites sprinkled the blood of the lamb on their doorposts in Egypt to elude the angel of death, they should be calling down upon themselves the guilt for the blood of the Lamb of God—who had come to help them elude death. The cause for this heavy assertion was very probably Matthew's realization that in 70 A.D. the Jews were dispossessed of their capital and that he saw it as a direct punishment for what their leaders had done there to Jesus.

Tragically, this one segment of one gospel has been the basis for two thousand years of unjustified anti-semitism.

LUKE: Whereas the other two begin the trial with an abrupt question from Pilate, Luke prefaces it with a more realistic statement of charges: (1) perverting the nation, (2) forbidding tribute, (3) claiming kingship—in effect, treason. And he hammers this home explicitly again and again throughout the remainder of his version of the trial. One of his major purposes, after all, is to convince his Gentile audience that Jesus was a spiritual not a political revolutionary. Three times Pilate explicitly and formally says he has found no crime in this man. Twice he has offered to chastise Jesus instead of crucifying him. (It is subtly ironic that he says he finds no crime in Jesus and *therefore* will chastise him.)

Luke has three repetitions of the charges and three definite statements from Pilate about Jesus' innocence: First, Pilate declares, "I find no crime in this man" (23:4). Was it perhaps a legal formula he was repeating? In any event he later states: "I do not find this man guilty of any of your charges against him. Neither did Herod. Nothing deserving death has been done by him" (vv. 14–15). And, finally, he says "I have found no crime in him deserving death" (v. 22, which Luke explicitly states is Pilate's third attempt).

Even in tiny touches, Luke stresses the guilt of the Jewish leaders over the guilt of the Roman leader. It was not Pilate who offered Barabbas but the Jews' own idea. And where Matthew and Mark say that Pilate "delivered him to be crucified," Luke specifies it with "Jesus he delivered up to their [the Jewish leaders'] will."

In all three it is heavily ironic that the Jews bring Jesus to Pilate on the charges of being a treasonous revolutionary and yet scream for a treasonous revolutionary—and murderer—in his stead. But it is Luke who inserts a repetition of Barabbas' treacheries at the very time of Jesus' sentencing.

Summary of Different Emphases

MARK

Mark is typically terse, only two-thirds the length of either of the other synoptics. He is abrupt as well, starting out right in the middle of the trial without any witnesses. If he knows about the death of Judas or the questioning by Herod, he doesn't mention it. And yet by his very brevity and abruptness, he somehow underlines the callousness of the people involved even more than the other evangelists who take more time with details.

MATTHEW

Matthew is more studied. He obviously has a theme of blood-guilt running through this whole section: first Judas, then Pilate, then the "people." But at least Judas and Pilate make some inept attempt at disassociating themselves from their guilt. The Jews are left with it, to their peril.

LUKE

Luke is the most studied of the three. He is careful to have the charges announced, and careful to have Pilate deny the charges three distinct times, each time in an official tone. He also joins Herod, the puppet Jewish king, with Pilate in finding no fault in this man. The scene is spare, like a Greek play: Pilate could be Creon, Jesus the condemned Oedipus, and the elders the Greek chorus.

Summary of Similarities

(1) The actors are generally the same (with the exception of Judas, Herod, Pilate's wife). The time is morning: the elders of the people hold a consultation and take Jesus off to Pilate.

(2) Pilate asks Jesus if he is the King of the Jews—each understanding something different by those words—and Jesus answers equivalently that he is. In all three, both the question and the answer are verbally identical. All three play on the loaded word "king," which could mean a purely religious messiah or a real threat to Caesar's power. (John will make it even more specific when he has the crowd cry out, "We have no king but Caesar!") In all three, Jesus' answer leaves the interpretation of the loaded word to Pilate who, by his subsequent actions with the crowd, surely seems to believe Jesus is not a political threat to Caesar.

(3) It is interesting to note that from his response to Pilate's first question Jesus does not utter another word until he has begun his trek to Calvary.

(4) In all three, Pilate releases a known revolutionary
and murderer named Barabbas instead of a man he
knows is falsely accused of being a revolutionary.
Three times Pilate tries to dissuade them, and in his
third attempt all three statements are verbally
identical. Finally, Pilate gives in to the crowd and
sends Jesus to be first scourged, then crucified.

Chapter Twelve

THE CRUCIFIXION

"Long live the King!"

Lest we get lost in details, checking small and large differences from text to text, recall that the passion account is an organic part of the whole gospel message—in fact its climax and fulfillment, both historical and historic. The core of that message of Jesus is the proclamation of the Kingdom—a totally new "world," completely counter to the accepted values of worldlings, even to the values of many dedicated and sincere Jews. Jesus has been edging toward this moment, this fulfillment, all through the gospel story: "It is at hand." It would be "in the midst of you," a spiritual change, a *metanoia*, a conversion, a complete about-face of one's values. And surely the Kingdom inaugurated by Jesus' passion is like no earthly Kingdom.

As we saw, Jesus' parables and proverbs and preaching were all warning that entrance into the Kingdom would mean a total reversal of one's previous values. In pages heavy with irony, the three evangelists underscore this "reversal message." If irony is a figurative means to say exactly the opposite of what one really expects, it is the perfect vehicle for the Christian message. Here is your king! He is poor, outcast, condemned, deserted. He is a king whose crown is made of thorns, and whose throne is a gibbet. It is a picture to confound the mind, a scandal to Jews and madness to Greeks. No wonder he is a confusion to literalists. No wonder he is a threat to materialists. The wonder is that pale agnostics can still dare to say, "What a nice man. What a fine model for conduct." The conduct he calls for if one is to find his Kingdom, as he does here, is an utter reversal of what one now thinks is truly important.

Outline

Because Matthew follows Mark with such remarkable closeness, we can treat the two together.

MATTHEW AND MARK	LUKE
A. Mockery by the Roman soldiers	
B. The Crucifixion —Simon of Cyrene —The crucifixion —Division of Jesus' garments	B. The Crucifixion —Simon of Cyrene —The women of Jerusalem —The crucifixion (with two others) —Division of Jesus' garments; "Father, forgive."

C. The Vigil
—Inscription; Drink
—Two fellow criminals
—Derision by
  —passersby
  —priests
  —two robbers
	C. The Vigil
	—Derision by
	  —The rulers
	  —Soldiers (inscription; drink)
	  —Two criminals
	  —The Good Thief

D. The Death —Darkness: noon to three —"My God, My God!" —Death —Curtain —Centurion —Women	D. The Death —Darkness: noon to three —Curtain —"Father, into thy hands!" —Death —Centurion —Women

The Mockery

MATTHEW 27

²⁷Then the soldiers of the govenor took Jesus into the praetorium, and they gathered the whole battalion before him. ²⁸And they stripped him and put a scarlet robe upon him, ²⁹and plaiting a crown of thorns they put it on his head, and put a reed in his right hand. And kneeling before him they mocked him, saying, "Hail, King of the Jews!" ³⁰And they spat upon him, and took the reed and struck him on the head. ³¹And when they had mocked him, they stripped him of the robe, and put his own clothes on him, and led him away to crucify him.

MARK 15

¹⁶And the soldiers led him away inside the palace (that is, the praetorium); and they called together the whole battalion. ¹⁷And they clothed him in a purple cloak, and plaiting a crown of thorns they put it on him. ¹⁸And they began to salute him, "Hail, King of the Jews!" ¹⁹And they struck his head with a reed, and spat upon him, and they knelt down in homage to him. ²⁰And when they had mocked him, they stripped him of the purple cloak, and put his own clothes on him. And they led him out to crucify him.

Unraveling the Meaning

- Judging from what we've seen of him so far, why would you suspect Luke omits this segment?

- The only real difference, other than the styles, is that Mark says they gave Jesus a purple cloak and Matthew says it was scarlet. Why is Matthew the more probably historical?

MARK / MATTHEW: The only noticeable difference between the two is that Mark speaks of a purple cloak (suggesting imperial robes) and Matthew, probably more correctly, changes it to the scarlet cloak which Roman legionaries wore. Purple was a color reserved for royalty, but the purpose of this ironic investiture is the same for both.

The scourging which preceded this event was not the "chastising" of Luke's version (a light beating as a warning for bad boys) but a beating with metal-tipped whips.

The praetorium both speak of was the headquarters of the Roman soldiers. The thorns would be the long thorns used for fires, and probably stored in the courtyard. These could have been woven into a circlet like the radiate crowns of Greek kings, similar to the one on our Statue of Liberty.

The mockery is a parody of the acclaim given to an emperor after a victory. To the soldiers, Jesus appears to be only another prisoner and a means to wile away the time in a bit of sadistic horseplay: If you want to be a king, we'll make you one! Their "game" expresses their contempt not only for this so-called king, but also for the people he "rules," whose little uprisings plague the lives of these soldiers.

Ironically, Jesus is actually proclaimed a king when he really is at the brink of fulfilling his kingly duty of inaugurating his King-dom. With a double-twist, the soldiers are using ironic sarcasm about Jesus, yet unbeknownst to them, it is the ironic truth.

LUKE: Although he knows of this incident from his copy of Mark, Luke omits the incident entirely. First of all, he has already had a mockery in Herod's court, and he wants his readers to realize that the blame was on the Jewish leadership and not on the Romans. Moreover, it is typical of him to spare Jesus the worst indignities if he can.

B. The Crucifixion

MATTHEW 27
32As they were marching out, they came upon a man of Cyrene, Simon by name; this man they compelled to carry his cross.

MARK 15
21And they compelled a passer-by, Simon of Cyrene, who was coming in from the country, the father of Alexander and Rufus, to carry his cross.

LUKE 23
26And as they led him away, they seized one Simon of Cyrene, who was coming in from the country, and laid on him the cross, to carry it behind Jesus. 27And there followed him a great multitude of the people, and of women who bewailed and lamented him. 28But Jesus turning to them said, "Daughters of Jerusalem, do not weep for me, but weep for yourselves and for your children. 29For behold, the days are coming when they will say,
'Blessed are the barren and the wombs that never bore, and the breasts that never gave suck!' 30Then they will begin to say to the mountains 'Fall on us'; and to the hills, 'Cover us.' 31For if they do this when the wood is green, what will

happen when it is dry?" ³²Two others also, who were criminals, were led away to be put to death with him.

³³And when they came to a place called Golgotha (which means the place of a skull), ³⁴they offered him wine to drink, mingled with gall; but when he tasted it, he would not drink it. ³⁵And when they had crucified him, they divided his garments among them by casting lots; ³⁶then they sat down and kept watch over him there.

²²And they brought him to the place called Golgotha (which means the place of a skull). And they offered him wine mingled with myrrh; but he did not take it. And they crucified him, and divided his garments among them, casting lots for them, to decide what each should take.

³³And when they came to the place which is called The Skull, there they crucified him, and the criminals, one on the right and one on the left. ³⁴And Jesus said, "Father, forgive them; for they know not what they do." And they cast lots to divide his garments. ³⁵And the people stood by, watching.

Unraveling the Meaning

- Simon of Cyrene comes into the story from out of nowhere. What would the fact that Mark knows the names of this "nobody's" sons suggest about Simon's later life?

- The beat which Luke inserts about the women of Jerusalem obviously comes from the "L" source. These women have come out to mourn Jesus' death. How does he, ironically, reverse the situation? Decompact the complex metaphor about the green wood and the dry wood.

- In none of the four gospels is there any mention of nails at the crucifixion scene. Where do we get the idea of nails?

- Luke twice mentions the criminals executed with Jesus. In the light of what he will do later in his version, can you guess why?

- Only Luke shows Jesus forgiving his executioners— and presumably "them" includes even those who brought it about. How is this typical of Luke?

MARK / MATTHEW are again almost verbally identical.

Simon of Cyrene is a puzzling character, coming as he does practically from nowhere, and yet with a known home town and with two sons. Cyrene is in North Africa near what is now Bengazi in Libya. Perhaps he was an emigrated Jew visiting the center of Judaism for Passover. It is suggested that he might have been converted, since his sons are known to Mark and presumably to his Roman audience. Matthew and Luke, however, writing in different places and for different audiences omitted their unknown names.

Normally the condemned prisoner carried only the crossbar of his cross, since the upright beam was a permanent fixture at the place of execution. But very likely, after the scourging with leaded whips, Jesus was weaker than his two fellow prisoners. Simon is a model of Christian discipleship, ready to help Jesus carry the burden of his cross and to share his sufferings. Simon is willing literally to "take up my cross and follow me."

The Aramaic word *gulgulta* means "skull," and the form we have is an attempt to render it into Greek. The Latin word for "skull" is *calvaria*, hence our word "Calvary." It is a grisly detail which all three share—though Luke bypasses the Aramaic approximation. (Note, too, that none of the gospels calls it a "hill"; it is just a "place.")

As we have seen before, this passage is a tissue of quotations from Psalms 69 and 22—the details of the gall, the division of garments, and later, the derision of the bystanders. Sour wine was often given to the condemned as a painkiller, frequently by ladies along his way as an attempt at compassion. The soldiers didn't mind, since the less their victim struggled, the sooner the job would be done. Luke mentions it later in v. 36.

Jesus refuses the painkiller, partly to refuse all supports in his lonely and deserted battle, partly perhaps to fulfill his own prophecy at the Last Supper that he would not drink wine again until he drank new wine in the Kingdom—which is now only three hours from fulfillment.

In all three cases, even in Mark who rarely shrinks from rude details, the crucifixion itself is stated in the fewest possible words: "They crucified him." There are no details so dear to preachers, like the ringing of the hammer blows and the blood. None of the four—including John—even mentions nails. (Hint: Think of doubting Thomas.) Jesus' nakedness is described only indirectly with references to the division of his garments. It is, after all, the painful degradation of their King.

LUKE is in substantial agreement with the others, paralleling the details of Simon of Cyrene, the place, the division of garments. He anticipates them by introducing Jesus' fellow criminals, and mentions them twice, because Luke will be the only one who has one of them speak to Jesus later and be forgiven. He postpones the offering of the sour drink. But Luke has two important and very typical additions.

The first is the women of Jerusalem. In general, Luke's gospel is more sensitive to women, not only showing them as

willing to accept discipleship but also, as here, being the only
ones with the courage to mourn Jesus publicly. The men are all
hiding out. Roman law forbade public mourning at the death
of a criminal, especially for one convicted of treason. Whether
the women are Christians is not clear, but their title "women of
Jerusalem" suggests they are not. Moreover, their function in
the scene is to act as a symbol of the Judaism which will, in fact,
suffer when the Romans destroy the city.

In Luke's eyes, the tragedy is not for Jesus; he is about to
inaugurate his Kingdom of reversal. The tragedy is on the side
of Israel. As at his arrest in Luke, Jesus is shown seeking not so
much to be consoled as to console. "The days are coming"
could be a prediction that Jerusalem is headed for literal
destruction, which Luke knows it was. But also the prophet
Hosea had spoken of Israel's predicament at being without a
king and then (10:8) predicted, "the idolatrous high places will
be destroyed. . . then they will say to the mountains, 'Cover us!'
and to the hills, 'Fall on us!'" It is typical apocalyptic imagery
for the End time and the inauguration of the new Kingdom.
And that is precisely what this moment is. If these are intended
as Christian women rather than, more literally, "daughters of
Jerusalem," it is also possible that Jesus was warning the church
that it, too, would suffer the same unjustified persecution as its
founder.

"If they do this when the wood is green. . . ." Green
wood burns with difficulty; dry wood burns quickly. If the
innocent Jesus meets the fate that these women see, what will
be the fate of those less worthy, those truly guilty of the values
of the Enemy's kingdom? As in much of Luke, this is an appeal
for their conversion, for their recognition of the true values.
The Passion is not meant as an occasion for sentiment or
resentment against those responsible for Jesus' sufferings and
death. "Weep not for me, weep for yourselves and for your

children." It is Jesus who is mourning for them! He is following the path of the Kingdom, and his countrymen are going in the opposite direction.

The second addition—again typical for Luke—is that Jesus, in the midst of this torment and desolation and apparent failure, is not thinking of himself but of his tormentors: "Father, forgive them." This is the Jesus who asked the unthinkable of his followers: turning the other cheek. Up till now, his innocence and dignity have been a silent judgment of his tormentors. Here, incredibly—according to the world's values—he forgives his torturers at the very moment they are torturing him. We will see even more of this in Luke in the next section.

C. The Vigil

MATTHEW 27	*MARK 15*	*LUKE 23*
37And over his head they put the charge against him, which read, "This is Jesus the King of the Jews." 38Then two robbers were crucified with him, one on the right and one on the left. 39And those who passed by derided him, wagging their heads 40and saying, "You who would destroy the temple and build it in three days, save yourself! If	25And it was the third hour, when they crucified him. 26And the inscription of the charge against him read, "The King of the Jews." 27And with him they crucified two robbers, one on his right and one on his left. 29And those who passed by derided him, wagging their heads, and saying, "Aha! You who would destroy the temple and build it in three	[See v. 38–inscription.] [Vv. 32, 33–other criminals.] [V. 37–"If you are King."]

you are the Son of God, come down from the cross!"

days, ³⁰save yourself, and come down from the cross!"

⁴¹So also the chief priests with the scribes and elders, mocked him, saying, ⁴²"He saved others; he cannot save himself. He is the King of Israel; let him come down now from the cross, and we will believe in him. ⁴³He trusts in God; let God deliver him now, if he desires him; for he said, 'I am the Son of God.'"

³¹So also the chief priests mocked him to one another with the scribes, saying, "He saved others; he cannot save himself. ³²Let the Christ, the King of Israel, come down now from the cross, that we may see and believe."

³⁵but the rulers scoffed at him, saying, "He saved others; let him save himself, if he is the Christ of God, his Chosen One!"

[See v. 48.]
[See v. 40.]
[See v. 37.]

[See v. 36.]
[See v. 30.]
[See v. 26.]

³⁶The soldiers also mocked him, coming up and offering him vinegar, ³⁷and saying, "If you are the King of the Jews, save yourself!"
³⁸There was also an inscription over him, "This is the King of the Jews."

⁴⁴And the robbers who were crucified with him also reviled him in the same way.

Those who were crucified with him also reviled him.

³⁹One of the criminals who were hanged railed at him, saying, "Are you not the Christ? Save yourself and us!" ⁴⁰But the other rebuked him, saying, "Do you not

fear God, since you
are under the same
sentence of condem-
nation? [41]And we
indeed justly; for we
are receiving the due
reward of our deeds;
but this man has done
nothing wrong." [42]And
he said, "Jesus,
remember me when
you come in your
kingly power." [43]And
he said to him, "Truly,
I say to you, today
you will be with me in
Paradise.

Unraveling the Meaning

- Mark says that the crucifixion began at the third hour, i.e., at nine in the morning. If Mark is right, how long did Jesus actually take to die?

- The derision from the crowd is focused not on Jesus as a rival to Caesar, for which he was condemned to death. What is the origin of those accusations?

- How is the crucifixion scene a parody of the episode of the transfiguration of Jesus? Think again of figurative language used as a negative instead of the photograph.

MARK has the same simple style, almost all sentences beginning with "And. . . ."

MATTHEW adds one more reference to Psalm 22 to the three in Mark, but the two accounts are again substantially the same.

Though there were undoubtedly others, Mark and Matthew mention only three taunts, each representative of a group and each focusing more clearly the meaning of the crucifixion.

In the taunts from the passersby—the ordinary Jewish citizens—the charge echoes from the Jewish trial about destroying the temple. This is ironic to the Christian reader, since Jesus—the new temple—is in fact being destroyed at this very minute. (Luke, who omits the charge from the trial, also omits it here.)

The second taunt, from the priests and elders, echoes the charge at the Roman trial about usurping kingship. It is also laced with ironies. It is a cynical admission that Jesus spent his whole public life doing nothing but helping the helpless, and now he himself is helpless. Then there is the equally scornful dare to come down from the cross as their much desired "sign," and then they will believe. Blindly, they do not see that, according to Yahweh's scriptural will, coming down from the cross would prove he was not the Messiah!

The third taunt, from the robbers, is not explained. It merely adds to the pathos of the state Jesus is in, reviled even by his fellow sufferers.

LUKE mentions the other "criminals" earlier, at the moment Jesus is crucified. His enthronement is a twisted, distorted picture of a king, to be sure, with two advisors on either side. It is an even more distorted picture of the Transfiguration, when Jesus stood in all his glory between Moses and Elijah. Kingship is the theme, and distortion here surely shows the difference between worldly values and the Kingdom's values. Companionship with sinners was Jesus' way of offering forgiveness.

In Matthew and Mark, Jesus speaks only once from the cross: "My God, my God, why have you forsaken me?" In Luke he speaks three times, and typically for Luke, they are speeches of mercy and dogged trust in the Father. The core of the gospel message is a reversal from the world's values. It struck me most strongly when I visited the ruins of Coventry Cathedral in England. It had been pounded unmercifully in World War II, and there was nothing left of it but an empty shell. But from the rough rubble, the townspeople had built an altar and behind it, from the half-burned beams, they had nailed together a bare, blackened cross. On the altar were only two words: "Father, forgive."

Luke repeats the same idea later on the lips of Stephen in Acts (7:60), the first of many Christian martyrs, and therefore, like his Master, a model of forgiveness even of his executioners. To see how rare such large-heartedness is, one need only read the daily actions of nations, businesses, big league athletics, ghetto crime, and on and on. There is only a small remnant, perhaps even within the organized churches, which can freely say, "Father, forgive." Reversal, indeed.

In Greek, the aorist tense of a verb means that the action is done once for all and is over with (i.e., "He said"); the imperfect tense, on the other hand, means an action is repeated over and over, like a habit or continuing action ("He was saying"). When Jesus said, "Father, forgive them," the verb is imperfect *(elegen)* which indicates that he was saying it over and over and over. It is a tiny detail, but significant. Far from being anti-semitic, far even from being ruthless with the Jewish leaders, Luke especially offers forgiveness to them.

In the revilings, Luke does not mention the passersby and restricts the revilings to the rulers, the soldiers, and one of the criminals. He is again at pains to focus the responsibility not on the common people as a nation but on their leaders. The "people" were watching (v. 35); the "leaders" were scoffing.

Note, too, the parallel with the temptations in the desert: "If you are the King of the Jews. . . . if he is the Christ of God . . . Are you not the Christ?" All are the same temptations for Jesus to doubt who he was which the Enemy had used before, in the desert. The Enemy, through his followers and those who accept his values, is using them again here. Here, the Enemy has control of both the religious and the civil "establishments."

Like a modern cinematographer, Luke establishes his scene with a wide shot of the rulers spread through the crowd, then tightens to the soldiers at the foot of the crosses, then focuses in on the criminals on either side of Jesus. But all of the taunts are variations of the same one: "If you're so big, pull off a miracle—while we watch."

Luke alone, again typically for the gospel of the Prodigal and the Good Samaritan, tells the story of the repentant criminal. Luke's is the gospel of great pardons. As he had done on the way to Golgotha with the women of Jerusalem, Jesus holds out hope even here in this hopeless place. With a reversal which one comes to expect in the gospels, it is from the mouth of a condemned criminal that the truth comes when he asks to be remembered in Jesus' Kingdom.

This moment sums up all of Luke's theology: We share the fate of Jesus, even though he is innocent and we are guilty of the values of the world. The turnabout, the conversion, will bring this treatment from the Enemy.

Rarely in the gospels is our Lord called by his name, "Jesus," which means "Yahweh is salvation." Twice in Luke it comes from those possessed by demons and crying out for mercy. Twice it is used when people cry out for healing. Here, too, it is a cry for mercy, for healing, for a savior—not in the taunting terms of the unrepentant thief but in humble faith.

In so doing, the "good thief" resolves the question that has underlain the trials and the taunts of Luke's Passion account: *"Who are you?"* With an act of faith, the least likely person in the scene declares that Jesus is the savior whose Kingdom is more real than the world.

Salvation comes in the very act of seeing and acknowledging that! Once again, Luke uses the techniques of Greek dramatists for whom the *anagnoresis* (i.e., the recognition) is the fullness of the *peripeteia* (i.e., the turning point, the conversion). By this they meant that the climactic turning point of a play like *Oedipus* occurs at precisely the moment when the truth finally erupts and must be acknowledged.

And, Jesus responds to the thief's recognition of his personal need for a savior. "Today you will be with me in Paradise." It will not be in some future End time, but today, immediately. The Kingdom begins at Jesus' death, not at the end of the world or when each of us dies. The Kingdom is *now*.

And the Kingdom consists of "being with" Jesus, not just in his retinue but "with" him; it is the difference between being "alongside" and being "inside."

It will be a "paradise," a word used in secular Greek literature to denote the private gardens of kings. It is also the word used of the place where Adam was at home with Yahweh. That state has returned—not in the literal sense of trees and snakes and serving girls, but in the symbolic sense of seeing values once again through Yahweh's eyes and not through the literalist eyes of the marketplace. Once again, symbols say more than literal language is able to.

At that moment of humble recognition, the good thief was in the Kingdom, in the reality which God sees and human beings can see only dimly, "through a glass, darkly."

D. The Death of Jesus

MATTHEW 27	MARK 15	LUKE 23
45Now from the sixth hour there was darkness over all the land until the ninth hour.	33And when the sixth hour had come, there was darkness over the whole land until the ninth hour.	44It was now about the sixth hour, and there was darkness over the whole land until the ninth hour, 45while the sun's light failed; and the curtain of the temple was torn in two.
46And about the ninth hour Jesus cried with a loud voice, "Eli, Eli, lama sabachthani?" that is, "My God, my God, why have you forsaken me?" 47And some of the bystanders hearing it said, "This man is calling Elijah." 48And one of them at once ran and took a sponge, filled it with vinegar, and put it on a reed, and gave to him to drink. 49But the others said, "Wait, let us see whether Elijah will come to save him."	34And at the ninth hour Jesus cried with a loud voice, "Eloi, Eloi, lama sabachthani?" which means, "My God, my God, why have you forsaken me?" 35And some of the bystanders hearing it said, "Behold he is calling Elijah." 36And one ran and, filling a sponge full of vinegar, put it on a reed and gave it to him to drink, saying, "Wait, let us see whether Elijah will come to take him down."	

⁵⁰And Jesus cried again with a loud voice and yielded up his spirit.

³⁷And Jesus uttered a loud cry, and breathed his last.

⁴⁶Then Jesus, crying with a loud voice, said, "Father, into your hands I commit my spirit!" And having said this he breathed his last.

Unraveling the Meaning

- Again, what is the symbolism of the torn curtain? Of darkness at noon?

- A thorny question: If Jesus had full possession of the divine knowledge, could he feel genuinely abandoned by God? Think back to the episode in the garden of olives: What was the symbolism of Mark's naked man running away?

- What is implied by the bystanders stopping the man with the sponge?

MARK'S only difference from Matthew is merely an apparent one: where Mark says, "Eloi, Eloi," Matthew says, "Eli, Eli." The discrepancy is explained by the fact that Mark was quoting Psalm 22:1 in Aramaic and Matthew was quoting it in classical Hebrew. Recall that this is the same psalm which both of them quoted earlier regarding the division of the virtuous man's garments and the crowds jeering at him. Here they quote the same psalm again: "My God, my God, why have you deserted me?"

It seemed clear that both Matthew and Mark were quoting the psalm previously and putting those details from the psalm into Jesus' situation—whether they happened historically or not—in order that the details of the narrative would themselves give a commentary on the historic meaning of this historical act

Did Jesus himself actually quote this psalm? Did Mark and Matthew put it into his mouth as a way of showing what this event truly was? Did the historical Jesus at that moment actually feel abandoned? Scholars I have read seem to prefer either the first or second rather than the third— namely, that either Jesus or the evangelists were making a comment with the psalm which would bring out the true meaning of the situation, rather than an actual decla- ration of inner abandonment. Surely, from Jesus' own mouth, we do have a stark underlining of the rightness of his taunters' accusations.

As a man of faith reading the Passion with the help of the evangelists and the scholars, I personally suspect that—whatever the words which were actually said—Jesus did actually feel doubt. It is true that in Luke, which is the gospel in which Jesus is so often tempted to doubt, this cry is omitted even though Luke has it available to him from his copy of Mark. But if Jesus was fully human, I cannot imagine him facing this test as serenely as the academicians would like to say he did. The whole point is tied up with the question of whether Jesus was only progressively aware of his own divinity and therefore faced, as all fully human beings must, the agonizing doubts about whether their self-assessments have been correct (See *Meeting the Living God,* Paulist, pp. 187–198).

Finally, Mark is the "gospel of challenge." He says with absolute bluntness: "See this? This is the worst. He has given of himself right to the bottom. Can you still believe?" The signs which Mark describes after Jesus' death are surely an indication that Jesus has not been abandoned. Surely, too, the testimony of the pagan centurion shows where Mark stands. But Mark hides nothing, not even the worst. And he says, "All right. There's the truth. Are you with us or not?"

Both **MATTHEW** and Mark are very similar otherwise.

The hours which all three speak of are not according to our clocks. Roman time was divided into watches during the night and hours during the day. Therefore, the "hours" do not begin until 6:00 A.M. Thus, the third hour is 9:00 A.M., the sixth hour is noon; the ninth hour is 3:00 P.M. (And the fabled "eleventh" hour of the parable is not an hour before midnight but an hour before quitting time.)

The darkness all three mention could be historical or not, without making much difference in the true symbolic meaning. It is the embodiment in nature of the near-triumph of Luke's "power of darkness."

There was a legend in Judaism that, since Elijah was the only one taken up to heaven while still alive (in a "fiery chariot"), he would return at the End time in order to aid the just in their need. You will recall that Luke has already shown Jesus saying more than once that John the Baptist was that Elijah. Here, however, Matthew follows Mark in associating this cry from the psalm with the apocalyptic events of the End time.

The bystanders mistake what Jesus says—which is under-standable, since a man who has endured such torture is not too articulate. One of them, perhaps out of compassion, runs to get Jesus a drink of sour wine. But here Mark and Matthew differ. Mark shows the man with the sponge himself saying, "Wait, let's see." Matthew has the others stop him. It is possible that Mark's man with the sponge was trying to keep Jesus alive long enough to see if Elijah would come! Either way, the cruelty goes on to the end, since they will not give him any relief—just in case the "big show" would happen if they let him suffer more.

Moreover, none of them says, "He died." He undoubtedly is dead, but it was not a *passive* yielding to the inevitable. Jesus is active to the end, and when he breathes his last it is an active rendering up of his spirit to the Father. His life does not slip away from him; he gives it. All three agree on that.

In Hebrew, Latin, and Greek, the word for spirit (the "I" which animates the body and mind) is the same as the word for breath. In the cosmic sense of the gospels, at this moment, Jesus gives up his own spirit to his new body—the Kingdom which from now on will be his presence and embodiment on earth.

LUKE'S only other difference is Jesus' loud cry, "Father, into your hands I commit my spirit!" It is the peaceful, resigned, fulfilled prayer of Psalm 31:4 and 5:

> "Pull me out of the net they have spread for me, for you are my refuge; into your hands I commit my spirit, you have redeemed me, Yahweh."

E. The Aftermath

MATTHEW 27	*MARK 15*	*LUKE: 23*
[51]And behold, the curtain of the temple was torn in two, from top to bottom; and the earth shook, and the rocks were split; [52]the tombs also were opened, and many bodies of the saints who had fallen asleep were raised, [53]and coming out of the tombs after his resur-rection they went into	[38]And the curtain of the temple was torn in two, from top to bottom.	[See v. 45—curtain.]

the holy city and
appeared to many.

54When the centurion
and those who were
with him, keeping
watch over Jesus,
saw the earthquake
and what took place,
they were filled with
awe, and said, "Truly
this was the Son of
God!"

39And when the
centurion, who stood
facing him, saw that
he thus breathed his
last, he said, "Truly
this man was the Son
of God!"

47Now when the
centurion saw what
had taken place, he
praised God, and
said, "Certainly this
man was innocent!"

55There were also
many women there,
looking on from afar,
who had followed
Jesus from Galilee,
ministering to him;
56among whom were
Mary Magdalene, and
Mary the mother of
James and Joseph,
and the mother of the
sons of Zebedee.

40There were also
women looking on
from afar, among
whom were Mary
Magdalene and Mary
the mother of James
the younger and of
Joses, and Salome,
41who, when he was in
Galilee, followed him,
and ministered to him;
and also many other
women who came up
with him to
Jerusalem.

48And all the multi-
tudes who assembled
to see the sight, when
they saw what had
taken place, returned
home beating their
breasts.
49And all his acquain-
tances and the
women who had
followed him from
Galilee stood at a
distance and saw
these things.

Unraveling the Meaning

- What purpose does Matthew have for "laying on the special effects"?

- Luke differs from Mark and Matthew in what the centurion says. From what you have seen so far, can you guess why?

- John's gospel says that the disciple John was with Mary at the foot of the cross. Which is the only synoptic who gives at least a hint that all the men were not cowards?

MARK, as we saw when we treated most of this segment previously, uses the declaration of the centurion as the climax of his gospel. In fact, he has never in his gospel used the term "Son of God" until this moment. In the context of the Kingdom theme of the Passion, it is meaningfully ironic that this Roman gives Jesus the imperial title *divi filius,* and the meaning to the Christian reader is even stronger.

MATTHEW, as we noted before, is the only one of the three who adds apocalyptic details beyond the rending of the temple curtain. This curtain was the one which hung before the holy of holies, the inner sanctum which only the high priest could enter. Whether the real curtain was torn or not is unimportant; the evangelists are saying God is no longer accessible only to the high priests! Access to God is open to any man or woman, through the death of Jesus Christ. The Mosaic cult has been superceded by a cult that will include even Gentiles. Judaism, not Jesus, has been vanquished at this moment. This is the destruction of the Temple—not by an act of war or by an abolition but by a replacement: "Another, not made by human hands" (Mark 14:58).

Only Matthew has the apocalyptic signs of the earthquake and the rising of the dead, as we have seen. Matthew makes the centurion's profession of faith a result of these signs; Mark, more impressively, makes it an act of faith in the person of Jesus rather than in the apocalyptic signs.

The women, whom all three evangelists describe, are used in Mark and Matthew as the "official witnesses" of Jesus' death—as they will be the first official witnesses of the resurrection. It is difficult, therefore, to say that the evangelists are radically anti-feminist. In the three synoptics—with the exception of Luke's vague phrase "all his acquaintances"—there is no mention of a single one of Jesus' male followers having the courage to be present at Jesus' death.

LUKE is far more controlled and briefer than the other two. He omits, with typical reluctance regarding apocalyptic, the apparent cries to Elijah, the earthquake, and the risen bodies. He lessens the claim of the centurion to a declaration of innocence—he had broken no Roman law. Given the situation, however, this is not a negligible claim. Notice, too, that only Luke shows that the centurion "praised God" before he made even this assertion—and without the provocation of any apocalyptic signs. The only portents Luke retains are the apparent eclipse and the torn curtain from Mark, and he uses them for the same reasons the others do: to place this event into a cosmic framework and to show that the Old Covenant has been replaced.

Only Luke shows many of the witnesses to the execution returning home "beating their breasts." This fits the theme of repentance and conversion which has surfaced frequently in his Passion account (Peter, the women of Jerusalem, the good thief).

The three evangelists, then, treat this same event from slightly different points of view. For Mark, the meaning of the Passion is that the Temple is through and a new temple has taken its place. For Matthew, this is a cosmic moment in which the forces of the Kingdom have, paradoxically, triumphed over the forces of the Enemy. For Luke, it is the moment when the Kingdom comes to existence in a change of heart in the people—which is an event as real and as cataclysmic as an earthquake.

Summary of Different Emphases

MARK-MATTHEW

Neither Mark nor Matthew hesitates to show the Roman guards making a fool of Jesus. Mark, after all, was writing for a Roman audience who could at any moment be called upon to undergo the same treatment. Matthew, writing for Jews, need have no fear of sharing the blame with Gentiles. More than Luke, they take care to select details from the Hebrew Scriptures to show that this ill-treatment of the Messiah should not only not be shocking but should indeed have been expected from the consistent pattern of Yahweh's dealings with his favorites.

Delicacy regarding the actual crucifixion is something one expects from Luke, but when all of the clinical details of the process are passed over in silence by both Mark and Matthew—who were only too aware of how it was done—we must draw some conclusions about their silence. It is a moment too great for words—even mythic words. Nonetheless, both give every group involved in the shameful scene its fair share of the blame: soldiers, priests, elders, and the whole "people" of Israel.

LUKE

Once again, Luke's is the "gospel of mercy." He exonerates the soldiers of the mockery and lays it on Herod and the Jewish elders. He shows Jesus taking pity on the women of Jerusalem, and he laments over the punishment this deed will inevitably visit upon them and on their children—not merely in the destruction of Jerusalem, but the treatment of Jesus by his Jewish countrymen did in fact give excuse for the persecutions and pogroms that God-fearing and mindless "Christians" will visit upon them and upon their children down to our own days. Even in his own pain, Jesus thinks of this meeting on the road as one more chance to call for a conversion of minds and hearts.

It is only Luke, a moment before the climax of his gospel, who shows Jesus uttering, over and over, the two words which sum up his message: "Father, forgive."

In the conversation between Jesus and the repentant criminal, Luke's gospel reaches its climax. This unlikely man hanging next to Jesus gives the answer to the question which has followed Jesus through his entire public life since the temptations in the desert: "Who are you?" And the answer is, I am Jesus, the savior. I will save you from the Kingdom of self-centeredness. In recognizing your need and my ability to answer your need, you are in the Kingdom. That recognition is the turning point, the conversion.

Finally, at the end, the inauguration of the Kingdom is not accompanied by the literal bizarre events. What those fearsome details in Matthew really mean is what Luke pictures more clearly: repentance over the old values and a total turnabout, a total conversion of the heart and mind.

Summary of Similarities

(1) All three evangelists agree about Simon of Cyrene following in Jesus' footsteps, sharing his cross. All agree about Golgotha, the refusal of a painkiller, the crucifixion without details, casting lots for Jesus' garments, the inscription proclaiming with terrible irony that Jesus is King of the Jews, the taunts of the bystanders, the two criminals crucified with him. They agree, too, on the time, the darkness, the curtain, the faith of the centurion, and the women who watch.

(2) The reviling, predicted in the psalms (and therefore a sign of the will of God), all show the same thing: the vicious contrast between Jesus' claims and Jesus'

present torment. The contrast is there for those who look at this event with the self-centered, literalist, and materialistic eyes of the Enemy's Kingdom. The cross was jarring to pious, faithful Jews and to sincere Gentiles as well. But to those who understand the mythic terms in which Yahweh has always described the real reality, this event is a triumph of love over self. Far more important, it is the moment essential for the resurrection, when our Brother entered the fulfillment of his mission: to free us from death and to share with us the aliveness of our Father.

Therefore, putting into the mouths of these people at the cross the very taunts with which Yahweh's enemies had reviled his Just One throughout Israel's history is criticism indeed. But it is absolutely typical of the wrenching reversal of values that the Kingdom requires and which we have seen is the core of Jesus' own message. If some of the details are fabricated or brought from somewhere else and inserted, they are surely in no way out of harmony with what Jesus himself actually said in his own words throughout his life.

(3) Throughout the three Passion accounts, Jesus has been hounded with taunts about his kingship. Ironically, this is precisely the moment Jesus becomes king—when he saves his people from the fear of death by dying himself. This is the man Matthew and Luke have shown as a baby receiving homage and gifts from humble Jewish peasants and from rich Gentile wise men. In this agony, Jesus is the embodiment of the paradox at the heart of his

message: "Unless a grain of wheat falls into the ground and dies, it cannot bear fruit."

But the drama is not yet over. We have seen only the climax. The Kingdom has just begun.

Chapter Thirteen

BURIAL AND EMPTY TOMB

The Gospel is a book of reversals. In the first century, it gave a complete turnabout to the literalist expectations about the Messiah. And from then till now, it calls for a 180-degree turnabout from the values of the world. But the events of this weekend mean far more than that. Its final chapter is the most shocking reversal of all: Jesus has died, and behold—he lives!

Outline

MATTHEW	MARK	LUKE
A. Joseph asks for body.	A. Joseph asks for body.	A. Joseph asks for body.
B. Shroud; rock tomb.	B. Shroud; rock tomb.	B. Shroud; rock tomb.
C. Women witness burial.	C. Women witness burial.	C. Women witness burial.
D. Jews ask for a guard.		
E. Morning after sabbath, women to anoint Jesus.	E. Morning after sabbath, women to anoint Jesus.	E. Morning after sabbath, women to anoint Jesus.
F. Earthquake; angel; guards like dead men.		
G. Angel.	G. Young man.	G. Two men.
H. They run in fear to tell the others.	H. They run in fear to tell the others.	H. They run in fear to tell the others.
I. Jesus meets them.		I. Apostles doubtful, but Peter runs to tomb.
J. Guards are bribed.		

The Burial

MATTHEW 27

⁵⁷When it was evening, there came a rich man from Arimathea, named Joseph, who also was a disciple of Jesus. ⁵⁸He went to Pilate and asked for the body of Jesus. Then Pilate ordered it to be given to him.

MARK 15

⁴²And when evening had come, since it was the day of Preparation, that is, the day before the sabbath, ⁴³Joseph of Arimathea, a respected member of the council, who was also himself looking for the kingdom of God, took courage and went to Pilate, and asked for the body of Jesus. ⁴⁴And Pilate wondered if he were already dead; and summoning the centurion, he asked him whether he was already dead. ⁴⁵And when he learned from the centurion that he was dead, he granted the body to Joseph.

LUKE 23

⁵⁰Now there was a man named Joseph from the Jewish town of Arimathea. He was a member of the council, a good and righteous man, ⁵¹who had not consented to their purpose and deed, and he was looking for the kingdom of God. ⁵²This man went to Pilate and asked for the body of Jesus.

⁵⁹And Joseph took the body, and wrapped it in a clean line shroud, ⁶⁰and laid it in his own new tomb, which he had hewn in the rock; and he rolled a great

⁴⁶And he bought a linen shroud, and taking him down, wrapped him in the linen shroud, and laid him in a tomb which had been hewn out of

⁵³Then he took it down and wrapped it in a linen shroud, and laid him in a rock-hewn tomb, where no one had ever yet been laid. ⁵⁴It was the day of

stone to the door of the tomb, and departed. [61]Mary Magdalene and the other Mary were there, sitting opposite the sepulchre.

the rock; and he rolled a stone against the door of the tomb. [47]Mary Magdalene and Mary the mother of Joses saw where he was laid. [Cf. 16:1]

Preparation, and the sabbath was beginning. [55]The women who had come with him from Galilee followed, and saw the tomb, and how his body was laid; [56]then they returned, and prepared spices and ointments. On the sabbath they rested according to the commandment.

Unraveling the Meaning

- Why such haste to get the body entombed?

- What does the fact that Joseph of Arimathea, someone we have never heard of before, takes the burden of Jesus' burial say about the other handpicked Twelve disciples?

- What does Pilate's surprise that Jesus was already dead say about the usual length of time a victim of crucifixion took to die?

- Why so much emphasis on the stone? And why the emphasis on the women who "saw where he was laid"?

- What evidence is there in Mark and Luke, as contrasted with Matthew, which shows that Mark and Luke were not writing for Palestinian Jews?

MARK and Matthew have a time for the burial which seems impossible. After sundown on Friday, the Sabbath has begun, and no orthodox Jew would dare to work, even in such an honorable cause. Rabbinical law allowed the care of a dead body but not the digging of a grave—thus the haste in securing the cadaver and walling it into a burial cave. Luke seems to have the more likely time sequence, mentioning evening approaching at the end of the work rather than at the beginning. If Jesus died around mid-afternoon, there was little enough time to secure Pilate's permission, remove the body, bury it and return home before the Sabbath began.

All three are quite similar in their treatment of Joseph of Arimathea. There are, however, a few tiny differences. Mark says he was a "respected" member of the council who was "looking for the kingdom of God," rather than expecting the literal fulfillment of the messianic prophecies as were many of his colleagues. Mark also inserts the note that asking for the body of Jesus took courage. In a very subtle way he underlines the fact that none of the men who had followed Jesus so closely for three years had that courage. Once again, the early church did not portray itself overgrandly. There is no "whitewashing" here. However, to do the apostles credit, the historical reason behind this event could well have been that Joseph was the most highly placed sympathizer they could find to negotiate with Pilate for Jesus' body.

Although all three use exactly the same words for Joseph's request to Pilate *(estato to soma tou Iesou)* and although Matthew and Luke both have Pilate turning over the *soma* (body) to Joseph, Mark—with typical bluntness—uses the word *ptoma* (corpse). The Jewish laws expressed in the book of Deuteronomy (21:23) forbade corpses to be left outside overnight.

Only Mark has Pilate expressing surprise that Jesus is already dead, since death by crucifixion often lasted two or three days.

Matthew and Mark emphasize placing the stone—and Matthew says a "great stone." Luke later speaks of a stone having been rolled back. This solidifies the barriers to the resurrection and eliminates claims that vandals had stolen the body.

More explicitly than the other two, Mark stresses the fact that the women are witnesses to the fact of the burial, along with Joseph. Further, though, it underlines the fact that more than one person was certain which tomb Jesus was actually buried in. There were countless tombs just outside the walls of Jerusalem. All three synoptics want to make very clear that there was no chance that the women went to the *wrong* tomb on Easter Sunday and found it empty. It is these same women who are witnesses to Jesus' death, to his burial, and to the empty tomb.

MATTHEW sticks very closely to Mark's version, streamlining somewhat by omitting some details, especially the ones which emphasize the work taking place after sabbath had begun. He does, however, note that Joseph is "rich" and does not mention that he was a member of the Council, the Sanhedrin, which had condemned Jesus. It is probable that, since he alone explicitly says that Joseph was a "disciple of Jesus," he either could not picture the Jewish trial with such a man remaining silent or he did not want to confuse his readers with a long explanation.

LUKE does make the clarification that Joseph, although a member of the Council, was a good and righteous man and had not voted to condemn Jesus. For the sake of his Gentile readers, Luke also clarifies that Arimathea was "a Jewish town."

Although Luke does not yet name the women, he does say that they returned to their homes to prepare the spices for later embalming and stresses explicitly that they would not break the Sabbath injunction against work. Thus, for his Jewish readers, he is showing that these women are law-abiding and therefore trustworthy witnesses.

The Guard at the Tomb (Matthew only)

MATTHEW 27

⁶²Next day, that is, after the day of Preparation, the chief priests and the Pharisees gathered before Pilate ⁶³and said, "Sir, we remember how the impostor said, while he was still alive, 'After three days I will rise again.' ⁶⁴Therefore order the sepulchre to be made secure until the third day, lest his disciples go and steal him away, and tell the people, 'He has risen from the dead,' and the last fraud will be worse than the first." ⁶⁵Pilate said to them, "You have a guard of soldiers; go, make it as secure as you can." ⁶⁶So they went and made the sepulchre secure by sealing the stone and setting a guard.

Unraveling the Meaning

- Since this episode is not in Mark, from what source did it come: Q, M, L?

- Whether or not this episode is historical, why does Matthew insert it? There is a connection between this and Matthew stressing that it was "a great stone."

- Considering where the disciples actually are at the moment, why is the priests' request ironic?

MATTHEW alone mentions this guard. It is odd in several ways. First, the Pharisees are shown recalling Jesus' predictions of the resurrection when his own disciples do not seem to. Second, although Pilate has been seen sneering at the Jews and their superstitions, he nonetheless grants a request he must have thought patently absurd—a man rising from the dead? Third, if there was a guard, historically, why would the other evangelists omit mention of it, since it would add one more obstacle that the resurrection could be shown to overcome? However, if this detail were added out of pious legend, there must have been a reason, and the only feasible one is that the Jews later claimed that the body of Jesus had indeed been removed by his disciples. If the Jews of Matthew's time actually did make that claim, however, it would be a clear indication that they, the "prosecution," had also checked the tomb and found it empty and therefore needed to trump up some other explanation for Jesus' body being missing.

The Empty Tomb

MATTHEW 28	MARK 16	LUKE 24
¹Now after the sabbath, toward the dawn of the first day of the week, Mary Magdalene and the other Mary went to see the sepulchre.	¹And when the sabbath was past, Mary Magdalene and Mary the mother of James, and Salome, bought spices, so that they might go and anoint him. ²And very early on the first day of the week they went to the tomb when the sun had risen.	¹But on the first day of the week, at early dawn, they went to the tomb, taking the spices which they had prepared.
²And behold, there was a great earth-	³And they were saying to one another, "Who	²And they found the stone rolled away

quake; for an angel of the Lord descended from heaven and came and rolled back the stone, and sat upon it. [3]His appearance was like lightning, and his raiment white as snow. [4]And for fear of him the guards trembled and became like dead men.

[5]But the angel said to the women, "Do not be afraid; for I know that you seek Jesus who was crucified. [6]He is not here; for he has risen, as he said. Come, see the place where he lay. [7]Then go quickly and tell his disciples that he is risen from the dead, and behold, he is going before you to Galilee; there you will see him. Lo, I have told you."

[8]So they departed quickly from the tomb with fear and great joy, and ran to tell his disciples. [9] And behold, Jesus met them and said, "Hail!" And they came up and took hold of

will roll away the stone for us from the door to the tomb?" [4]And looking up, they saw that the stone was rolled back; for it was very large. [5]And entering the tomb, they saw a young man sitting on the right side, dressed in a white robe; and they were amazed.

[6]And he said to them, "Do not be amazed; you seek Jesus of Nazareth, who was crucified. He is risen, he is not here; see the place where they laid him. [7]But go, tell his disciples and Peter that he is going before you to Galilee; there you will see him, as he told you."

[8]And they went out and fled from the tomb; for trembling and astonishment had come upon them; and they said nothing to any one, for they were afraid.

from the tomb, [3]but when they went in they did not find the body. [4]While they were perplexed about this, behold, two men stood by them in dazzling apparel;

[5]and as they were frightened and bowed their faces to the ground, the men said to them, "Why do you seek the living among the dead? He is not here, but has risen. [6]Remember how he told you while he was still in Galilee, [7]that the Son of man must be delivered into the hands of sinful men, and be crucified, and on the third day rise."

[8]And they remembered his words, [9]and returning from the tomb they told all this to the eleven and to all the rest. [10]Now it was Mary Magdalene and Joanna and Mary the

his feet and worshipped him. [10]Then Jesus said to them, "Do not be afraid; go and tell my brethren to go to Galilee, and there they will see me." [11]While they were going, behold, some of the guard went into the city and told the chief priests all that had taken place. [12]And when they had assembled with the elders and taken counsel, they gave a sum of money to the soldiers [13]and said, "Tell people, 'His disciples came by night and stole him away while we were asleep.' [14]And if this comes to the governor's ears, we will satisfy him and keep you out of trouble." [15]So they took the money and did as they were directed; and this story has been spread among the Jews to this day.

mother of James and the other women with them who told this to the apostles; [11]but these words seemed to them an idle tale, and they did not believe them. [12]But Peter rose and ran to the tomb; stooping and looking in, he saw the linen cloths by themselves; and he went home wondering at what had happened.

Unraveling the Meaning

- Where is the actual resurrection described? If they had described it, the gospel writers—especially Matthew—could have had a Spielberg holiday with it. It just begs for description. Why did they refuse to do that?

- Again, what comment does this new situation make about the men in Jesus' community?

- Each of the three has a different herald to tell the women that Jesus is risen: Mark has a young man wrapped in a white robe; Matthew has an angel; Luke has two men in dazzling apparel (John has two angels). Why the difference? (a) Recall in our discussion of symbols about the meaning of angels. What do they symbolize? (b) Recall at the Sanhedrin trial that the elders were trying to come up with two witnesses who would agree on their testimony. What could that have to do with Luke and John doubling the heralds?

- Is there a reason why Matthew includes an actual meeting with Jesus and the others omit it? Again, remember that Matthew is writing for potential Jewish converts and that he alone had shown the priests requesting a guard.

Note that in none of the versions is the resurrection itself described. Actually, their silence is one more argument in favor of their truthfulness. If they were out to hoax their readers, they could have done a bang-up job, as we can see from other epics of their time and later. What's more, they did not hesitate to picture their own "heroes," the apostles, cringing in fear while the women fearfully witness the crucifixion, the burial, and the empty tomb. That very honesty about their cowardice also underlines the dramatic change that came about among them: The cowards of this weekend turned around 180 degrees two months later and stood up fearlessly proclaiming the Kingdom. They went to their deaths refusing to back down. They testified that the reason for that total conversion was that they had seen Jesus alive again.

MARK, unlike the other two synoptics, shows the women on the way to the tomb wondering how they will move the stone. It is odd that, although they had seen it in place and had been forced to remain away a whole day presumably pondering it, that they didn't think of this before they set out to the graveyard. It is at least possible that Mark is quietly underlining the fact that only these women—and none of the men—were willing to come even this close to identification with Jesus and his dangerous teachings. Mark doesn't say how the stone was actually removed; they simply arrive and find it done.

As we have seen before, the young man (*neaniskos*) of this passage may echo back to the young man who deserted Jesus in that puzzling little addition to Mark's version of the arrest. The second book of Maccabees (3:26 and 33) uses a white-robed young man as a symbol of an angel or of the presence of God's message, and white robes are frequently used as symbols for heavenly visitations—as with Jesus himself at the Transfiguration.

Just as the symbols of the heavenly presence are different in each version, the speech of the messenger(s) is different—although each says exactly the same thing beneath the differing wording: "He is risen; he is not here." Unlike the other two synoptics, Mark shows the messenger sending the women not only to the disciples but expressly to Peter. If Papias is correct and Mark was indeed Peter's interpreter, this specific inclusion is understandable. In the light of Peter's denials, it is also quietly critical of him that Peter, the boaster, should not be here with these courageous women.

The statement that the women said "nothing to anyone" obviously does not mean that the women refused to tell the story even to the apostles, since they had just been given a mission from God. Rather, it means that they told no one else.

There are some who argue that the original version of Mark's gospel ended right here at verse 8. The vocabulary and style of the rest of Chapter 16 seem to some scholars to be too different from Mark's usual language, and they argue that the rest of Mark's gospel (16:9–20) was added perhaps as late as 100 A.D. This would account for the strong divergences in the remaining sections of Matthew and Luke—not having Mark as a common source. Moreover, it could be typical of the brusqueness of Mark to end right there, saying equivalently, "See! They went to the tomb and he was gone! Now—what do you think?"

However, this would have the whole gospel end with the Greek conjunction *gar* ("For . . . ") which seems highly unlikely. Furthermore, the Council of Trent (1546) resolved the question by declaring that the ending of Mark's gospel as we have it today (16:9–20) is indeed to be accepted with the same validity as the rest of Mark's gospel.

MATTHEW says nothing of anointing, and thus he avoids the problem of the women coming without considering how they would get into the tomb. The women came merely "to see the sepulchre."

The earthquake and the angel are, like Matthew's treatment of the crucifixion, apocalyptic symbols which put this moment into the same symbol-matrix as the book of Daniel. Unlike

Luke, Matthew doesn't use the explicit title "Son of man," but his symbols do that for him. Although Mark and Luke use less dramatic terms than "angel," the radiant white clothing in both of the other versions leaves no doubt that they were using exactly the same symbolism as Matthew.

The most striking difference in Matthew from the others is the actual appearance of Jesus to the women as they were running to tell the apostles. In Mark's version of the story, Jesus appears first to Mary Magdalene "from whom he had cast seven devils." Luke's version shows Jesus appearing first to two disciples on the road to Emmaus. John shows Jesus appearing first to Magdalene who, at first, confuses him with a gardener. But in all the versions Jesus appears to others before he appears to his eleven chosen apostles. One might say that the purpose is to show Jesus giving this reward to those who not only kept faith in him but had the courage of their convictions, even though he was still willing to give the less courageous another chance. It is worth noting that in Matthew the words of Jesus are substantially the same as the message of the angel.

Matthew is the only one to describe the priests bribing the guards, since he is the only one who describes their being posted at the tomb. It seems that since these soldiers might have gotten into trouble with Pilate as the result of sleeping on duty, this was a Roman guard rather than a Jewish group. They have come to the most interested parties to get them off the hook—and they have chosen well. Obviously, Matthew inserts this story to combat the rumors going around in his own time that, although the tomb was indeed empty, it must have been Jesus' disciples who spirited the corpse away—"and this story has been spread among the Jews to this day."

LUKE: This section and the rest of the gospel of Luke (24:1–53) all take place on a single day. If we had had only Luke's version, we would have no knowledge of a forty-day period of appearances by Jesus. As the *JBC* says, "This is the first day of a new age—Sunday—which the Church will set apart as its new Sabbath of heavenly rest and joy" (44:175).

The bearer of the news of the resurrection in Mark is a young man; in Matthew, an angel; in John, two angels; in Luke, two men in white. This difference in symbols is only surface; all four are using different symbols to express exactly the same reality. Each is making a symbolic attempt to embody the presence of a message from God—which, of course, is not physical itself. The use of men in dazzling white garments as symbols of this presence is also used by Luke elsewhere in both his gospel and his book of Acts (Luke 11:36, 17:24, and Acts 1:10, 9:3, 10:30, 22:6). There is also an echo of Luke's version of the transfiguration (9:29) when the divinity of Jesus is expressed by his being clothed in garments "brilliant as lightning," standing with two heavenly witnesses (as here at the tomb).

The message at the tomb in Luke is far simpler than the other two versions: "Why do you seek the living among the dead?" There is the gospel message in a nutshell: Jesus lives.

Matthew and Mark show the heavenly messenger directing the disciples to meet Jesus in Galilee, whereas Luke does not. This is in keeping with the whole geographical thrust which gives shape to his double narrative in his gospel and the Acts. The message began in Galilee and moved inexorably toward fulfillment during a single journey up to Jerusalem (Luke's gospel); then it moved equally inexorably away from Jerusalem to Rome (Luke's Acts of the Apostles). There is no turning back. The whole movement of God's plan is from Galilee to the Jews and then, leaving Judaism behind, to the whole world.

Luke uses this occasion to insist that the Easter event be seen in light of the prophecies about the Messiah and by the Messiah. The Son of Man of Daniel = the Suffering Servant of Isaiah = Jesus. It had been repeated over and over in the revelation of God's way of doing things that the Messiah was one who must suffer and die in order to save his people. It had been the way of God with Israel. Jesus had prophesied that it would be the way of God with him. Suffering, dying and being reborn are "the way things are"—which is the same as saying the will of God. And, very simply put, this is also the role each Christian is called on to live: to suffer the tension between the world's values and the Kingdom's values, to die to the world and to be rejuvenated in the Kingdom.

Summary of Different Emphases

The differences are almost all surface ones. The only large differences occur in Matthew who inserts the two episodes with the guards, apparently to combat rumors circulating in Palestine in his own time that—although the body of Jesus was indeed gone from its burial place—there were this-world explanations. He confronts this attack with evidence that the guards were bribed to spread such rumors by the unprincipled priests.

At first reading, the most startling difference in the four versions is the fact that each has a quite different way of announcing the fact that the tomb is empty: a young man, an angel, two men, two angels. However, anyone with a knowledge of symbolic language and the use to which we have seen it consistently put in the gospels should find no real difficulty with this. The author of Genesis pictured the heavenly presence to Adam as a friend who strolled in his garden. The author of Exodus pictured this presence as a burning bush. Even a non-believer, if he or she has ever been in love, knows that there are experiences and realities which defy being put into words. Only symbols—no matter how inadequate—will suffice.

Therefore, Mark with his puzzling *neaniskos,* Matthew with his apocalyptic earthquakes and angel, and Luke with his two dazzling witnesses are using different symbols to express exactly the same reality: Yahweh has vindicated Jesus by raising him from the dead. These witnesses are surprisingly different to one unacquainted with the full gospel of each author. But even anyone who has seen only the Passions in parallel as we have in these pages can see that the choice of these particular symbols by each evangelist is obviously typical. Mark has used his *neaniskos* for this same purpose before; Matthew has favored apocalyptic thunder and earthquake and angels for this same purpose before; Luke has preferred shining garments and double witnesses for this same purpose before.

Summary of Similarities

Beneath these surface differences, the three evangelists declare exactly the same truth: Jesus was raised from the dead. Moreover, even the details of the versions are remarkably the same. A highly placed Jew named Joseph of Arimathea, who was hospitable to the preaching of Jesus, went to Pilate and secured permission to take Jesus' body down from the cross and bury it. Accompanied by women followers of Jesus, he wrapped it in a linen shroud, placed it in a tomb hewn out of rock, and rolled a stone in front of the doorway. The women noted carefully where the tomb was and then returned to their homes to keep the Sabbath.

At dawn on Sunday, after the Sabbath was over, these women—who included Mary Magdalene and another Mary—went to the tomb and found the stone rolled back from the doorway. They experienced a certainty of the divine presence who assured them that Jesus was indeed risen from the dead and that the tomb was indeed empty. They realized, with certainty, that Jesus had told them all along that exactly this would happen, and they returned in haste to tell the others.

Although each of the synoptics diverges from the others on some details more sharply than we have seen in the Passion, one thing is clear: The apostolic church apparently saw no need to harmonize these differences—in effect, to choose from the many versions in order to have one happy, consistent story. The resurrection is the most stunning event of the New Testament, and indeed of all time. Had any group of us been witness to the empty tomb, a similar difference of recollection regarding details would have been just as inevitable. And if they—who faced the lions for their stubborn clinging to the truth of the resurrection—were not troubled by these differences, then neither should we.

Luke's next volume, Acts, will show the break of Jesus' disciples, not from the Hebrew Scripture, but from the Hebrew law and its ways.

> "Then Peter addressed them: 'The truth I have now come to realize' he said 'is that God does not have favorites, but that anybody of any nationality who fears God and does what is right is acceptable to him.
>
> 'It is true, God sent his word to the people of Israel, and it was to them that the good news of peace was brought by Jesus Christ—but Jesus Christ is Lord of all. You must have heard about the recent happenings in Judea, about Jesus of Nazareth and how he began in Galilee, after John had been preaching baptism. God had anointed him with the Holy Spirit and with power, and because God was with him, Jesus went about doing good and curing all who had fallen into the power of the devil. Now, I and those with me can witness to everything he did throughout the countryside of Judea and in Jerusalem itself, and also the fact that they killed him by hanging him on a tree, yet three days afterwards God

raised him to life and allowed him to be seen, not by the whole people but only by certain witnesses God had chosen beforehand. Now, we are those witnesses—we have eaten and drunk with him after his resurrection from the dead—and he has ordered us to proclaim this to his people and to tell them that God has appointed him to judge everyone, alive or dead. It is to him that all the prophets bear this witness: that all who believe in Jesus will have their sins forgiven through his name' " (Acts 10:34–43).

There, in six sentences from the model disciple, you have the whole thing.